The Librarian's Legal Companion

The Librarian's Legal Companion

JONATHAN S. TRYON

G.K. Hall & Co.
An Imprint of Macmillan Publishing Company
NEW YORK

Maxwell Macmillan Canada
TORONTO

Maxwell Macmillan International
NEW YORK OXFORD SINGAPORE SYDNEY

G. K. Hall & Co.
An Imprint of Macmillan Publishing Company
866 Third Avenue
New York, NY 10022

Maxwell Macmillan Canada, Inc.
1200 Eglinton Avenue East, Suite 200
Don Mills, Ontario M3C 3N1

Macmillan Publishing Company is part of the Maxwell Communication Group of Companies

Library of Congress Catalog Number: 93-39607

Printed in the United States of America

Printing Number
1 2 3 4 5 6 7 8 9 10

Library of Congress Cataloging-in-Publication Data
Tryon, Jonathan S.
    The librarian's legal companion / Jonathan S. Tryon.
    p. cm.
    Includes index.
    ISBN 0-8161-1961-9. — ISBN 0-8161-1962-7 (pbk.)
    1. Library legislation—United States. 2. Librarians—Legal status, laws, etc.—United States. I. Title.
KF4315.T79 1994
344.73'092—dc20
[347.30492]   93-39607
                                                                        CIP

The paper used in this publication meets the minimum requirements of American National Standard for Information Sciences—Permanence of Paper for Printed Library Materials.
ANSI Z39-1984. ♾ ™

*To My Wife, Jean, whose help, support, encouragement,
and love have been constant*

Contents

ACKNOWLEDGMENTS   ix

INTRODUCTION   xi

1   PREMISES LIABILITY   1

Negligence   2
What Duty Is Owed   4
Abolition of the Categories   8
Governmental Immunities   9
Other Defenses   11
Liabilities in Failure to Protect
     Against Acts of Third Parties   12
Liability for Some Intentional
     Torts   13

2   DISCRIMINATION IN EMPLOYMENT   17

The Equal Pay Act of 1963   18
Title VII   26
Sexual Harassment   36
Age Discrimination in Employment Act   45
Americans with Disabilities Act   56

3   EMPLOYMENT SECURITY   77

Employment-at-Will   78
Public Sector Employment   82
Collective Bargaining   86

4   PRIVACY IN THE WORKPLACE   103

5   CENSORSHIP   117

6 COPYRIGHT   137

INDEX OF CASES   161
GENERAL INDEX   165

Acknowledgments

Probably every author, whether of fiction or nonfiction, owes a debt of gratitude to librarians. With this particular work concerning matters of a legal nature, I am beholden especially to the people of the Rhode Island Supreme Court Law Library, which is led brilliantly by Kendall Svengalis with the marvelous assistance of Sondra Giles, the Deputy Law Librarian, and Karen Quinn and Colleen Hanna, who cover public service with the support of Catherine Antuono and Martha Moore. These people are truly professional in their knowledge of legal materials, and their dedication to public service is unexcelled. This work could not have been done without their help and I cannot possibly repay the debt I owe them. What is most impressive to me, however, is that every patron who enters the facility—lawyer, student, or ordinary citizen—gets the same high level of service. To those librarians I say thank you both for your help to me personally and for your inspirational example of what public service ought to be.

Every teacher owes a debt of gratitude to students also. Many were assigned readings from various stages of the manuscript of this work and many offered useful suggestions and criticism. I would particularly like to single out Kathleen Leonard, Jean Shepard, and Claudia Mayer for their very substantive contributions.

Finally, I must express my overwhelming gratitude to my daughter, Julia R. Tryon, who is a reference librarian at Providence College. One cannot say enough about the value of having a reference librarian in the family and particularly one who is conversant with the vagaries of the personal computer. Her assistance was truly invaluable.

Kingston, Rhode Island

Introduction

In a litigious society such as ours any enterprise must be aware of the legal consequences of its actions and every employee has both the right and the duty to know his or her legal standing as an employee. It is the purpose of this work to provide an introduction to those areas of the law that are particularly applicable to libraries, although much of what is covered here is applicable to any employment situation. While certain specialties such as sports law and education law exist and continue to evolve there is no specialty known as "library law." What is presented here are those areas of law with which librarians ought to be familiar.

It is true, of course, that libraries as enterprises and librarians as individuals are exposed to all areas of the law as is any enterprise or individual. Theoretically there is no limit to the subject matter appropriate for this work and one could argue that therefore there ought to be consideration of contracts, torts in greater depth, property law, and perhaps criminal law besides those areas that are offered here. However, it is not the intent of this work to provide a comprehensive treatise of all areas of the law that might impinge on libraries and librarians, but to discuss those areas that are likely to do so.

Caveats

When I started law school I was pleased to think that, at last, I would learn what the law was. What I did learn, however, was that the law is a constantly shifting sea of decisions in which general principles can, usually, be discerned but that at no time can one say absolutely, definitively, and without contradiction that such and such is the law. Every situation has its own peculiarities, and when brought to court, prompts a decision that is applicable to the particular case but is slightly skewed in its application to a slightly different set of facts. The result is that one can present a whole panoply of cases suggesting a particular interpretation of the law but that with any particular set of facts a court might decide differently. The function of a lawyer in a trial situation is to convince the court or jury that the facts favor the particular client. It is a very interesting approach to the determination of truth but it means that any writer discussing the interpretation of law can, at best, speak only in terms of probability. Some things are better established than others, of course, but the one sure thing in law is that nothing is certain.

It is my intent in this work to state what the law is at the present time and not what the law ought to be. This is not a polemical work and I have avoided arguing any particular point of view. It is true that some of the topics included here, such as sexual harassment, engender strong reactions, and it may be concluded by some that a failure to show strong feelings on an issue is proof that you are in the other camp. This is unavoidable in a work whose purpose, as I have said, is to say what the law is but I would not like readers to think that I have no opinion on the issues.

One final caveat: this work is not a substitute for a good lawyer nor will it make anyone into a lawyer. Nor is it a substitute for the detailed treatises that each of the topics covered has called forth over the years, the important ones having been cited in the following sections. It is meant to be an introduction to the legal aspects of the topics included, accessible to readers without legal expertise, convenient in a single volume. One hopes that all the facts and interpretations are correct as stated but facts can be elusive and interpretations are always debatable.

Jurisdictions

While it is surely true that nothing is certain, the matter is greatly complicated by the fact that each state has its own understanding of what the law is, which makes generalizations about the law rather hazardous. To compound the problem, there is the federal court system, which may reach different conclusions on a particular set of facts than would a state court. This is not the place to discuss the effect of the supremacy clause of the United States Constitution nor is there space to discuss the question of state versus federal courts as a forum for deciding disputes. However, it cannot be stressed strongly enough that one must be aware of the law in one's own state, if the matter is not one of a federal question. The courts of one's own state care only about their own precedents, and only when a question has not previously been presented will a decision from another jurisdiction be persuasive.

Citations

Lawyers love citations and any reader of law reviews will often find more space devoted to citations than to the article itself. In this work there is no attempt to buttress every possible legal contention with a citation, but rather to indicate those cases that substantiate the particular point being made without an exhaustive (and exhausting) listing of all possibly relevant cases. What follows here is a brief introduction to legal citation detailed only enough to allow the absolute neophyte access to the material cited herein. It is most certainly not a substitute for a course in legal research. Short of taking such a course readers might find useful one of the many guides to legal research. One such is Morris Cohen and Kent Olson's *Legal Research in a Nutshell* (St. Paul, MN: West, 1992), which is updated regularly, inexpensive, and comprehensive enough for most purposes.

The actual system of citation used here is a hybrid of the system set forth in *A Uniform System of Citation*, published by the Harvard Law Review Association, and the *Chicago Manual of Style*. Thus legal citations are given as they appear in cases and nonlegal citations appear in a normal format.

The vast majority of legal citations deal with cases or decisions and follow a uniform format: given first is the name of the case followed by the volume number in which the case appears. Next comes an abbreviation indicating the level or jurisdiction of the particular court that decided the case. This is followed by the first page of the case and, usually, the date the case was decided. Thus, for example, *Bratt v. International Business Machines Corp.*, 785 F.2d 352 (1986) indicates that the case named appeared in volume 785 of the federal reporter, second series, beginning on page 352 and it was decided in 1986.

For the uninitiated there is a problem in recognizing the particular court being cited. Experience, of course, solves this but a useful guide to the abbreviations can be found in the front matter of each volume of the *United States Code Service*. It is also useful to recognize the extent of the particular court's jurisdiction. As a general rule, United States Supreme Court decisions carry the most weight, followed by federal courts of appeal, but this depends upon which law a particular case relies. The United States Supreme Court interprets the U.S. Constitution while each state supreme court interprets its own state's constitution, often with different results. For example, the U.S. Supreme Court has found roadblocks to detect drunk drivers to be constitutionally sound, but the Rhode Island Supreme Court has found such roadblocks a violation of the Rhode Island Constitution. The matter of finding cases is muddied by the fact that there are multiple sources for the cases in some, but not all, instances. United States Supreme Court cases are reported in three different places: the official *United States Reports*, the *Supreme Court Reporter*, published by West, and *United States Reports, Lawyers' Edition*, published by the Lawyers' Co-op. Seemingly overkill, the latter two each provide very useful additional information and most lawyers are pleased to have access to all three.

Decisions of the lower federal courts are found, for the Courts of Appeal, in the Federal Reporter, now in its Third Series, which is abbreviated F.3d. Decisions of the Federal District Courts are reported, when they are reported and not all are, in the Federal Supplement abbreviated F.Supp. Both of these are West publications.

Decisions of state appellate courts usually show up in two places. A majority of the states still have their own series of reports and the key to their identification will be the state's abbreviation between the volume and page numbers. In addition, each state's appellate decisions are reported in what is known as the National Reporter System, published by West. In this system various states are grouped in generally logical geographical arrangements. For instance, the *Northeastern Reporter* includes decisions from Massachusetts, New York, Ohio, Indiana, and Illinois. The *Pacific Reporter* includes the western states, many of which, such as Kansas and Oklahoma, would be surprised to be considered a part of the Pacific Rim, but still, the system works. For those with computer access, the whole business is online through such databases as LEXIS and WESTLAW.

1

PREMISES LIABILITY

Considering the size of monetary awards won in court cases, it would be prudent to run any operation with a degree of care that will minimize the chances of incurring a lawsuit. Moreover, there is a moral (though not necessarily legal) imperative to keep our fellow creatures from harm. While it is undoubtedly the majority view that people should base their conduct on what is the right thing to do rather than out of fear of legal retribution, it still should be useful for any administrator to have an idea of what the *law* thinks is the right thing to do so that appropriate measures may be instituted in light of this. This chapter will discuss the tort liability that a library may incur when harm befalls persons while in or on library property. The purpose is twofold: one, to provide information that will allow an administrator to enact proper procedures, including the possible costs for failure to do so; and two, to give the administrator some idea of what his or her lawyer will be talking about when, in spite of all the best efforts, a patron is harmed and sues the library.

Specifically, the matters covered here will be the duty of care and what care is owed to whom, the concept of negligence, the obligation to protect patrons from the crimes or other harms of third parties, the risks involved in trying to protect library property, and some of the defenses to the tort of negligence, including governmental immunity. This chapter will not discuss the duty owed to the library's employees, such as safety in the workplace, nor will it include any discussion of negligence in the provision of information—malpractice of librarianship, one might suppose it would be called. This seems to be a recurring fear in the minds of reference librarians, but as yet there have been no reported cases. Finally, strict liability, that is, liability without fault, will not be discussed as libraries are not likely to be in a position where such liability is applicable.

As noted in the introduction, this work cannot cover in great depth the various topics selected. Those wishing more depth of discussion than can be covered here will find the following sources useful: Joseph A. Page, *The Law of Premises Liability*, 2d ed. (Cincinnati: Anderson Publishing Co., 1988 with 1991 Supplement); W. Page Keeton, *Prosser and Keeton on the Law of Torts* (St. Paul: West Publishing Co., 1984 with 1988 Supplement); F. Harper, F.

James, and O. Gray, *The Law of Torts* (Boston: Little, Brown, 1986 with 1989 Supplement).

Two things should be noted at the outset: the law in this area, as in most areas, is complicated and it is not possible to include here all the finer points relevant to the matter. The Page work, above, which deals directly on the subject, is over 400 pages long; the Keeton and Harper works, which have a broader scope, are 1,200-plus pages and six (fat) volumes respectively. What follows, then, is a general outline of the law. In reading this outline, it must be remembered that each state has developed its own traditions and interpretations of the law so, while general outlines can be drawn, any particular point may not apply in a particular state. This could be critical if a library is brought to court. It may be worth reiterating that there is no particular category of law for libraries; thus, premises liability for libraries is the same law that applies to any premises.

Negligence

Centuries ago it was the understanding of the English common law that if a person was harmed, some recompense was due him regardless of whether there was fault or not or whether there was some special relationship established between the perpetrator and the one harmed. The nineteenth century saw the gradual development of a requirement of fault as essential to a negligence case. This fault may arise either from an act that should have been done but wasn't, or one that should not have been done but was. What one should or should not do is the heart of the matter, but it is complicated by the question of whether the person harmed had a right to protection from that harm.

Before we go further, it might be noted that many harms are considered to be without fault even though, in fact, every harm can be avoided. Often called the unavoidable accident or a "mere misadventure," a given accident could have been avoided by not undertaking the activity in the first place. Although a man who has a heart attack while driving a car and causes harm to another would not be found to have fault (unless, of course, he knew he was going to have the attack), he could have avoided the accident by simply not driving at all. Indeed, all traffic accidents could be halted by halting all traffic. All activity carries some risk of harm, but to cease activity out of fear of harm would induce absolute paralysis. Therefore, the law will not assign fault in many cases where actual harm has been done.

With this as prologue we will next look at the elements of a cause of action in a negligence case.

1. There has to be a duty or obligation recognized in law requiring a certain standard of conduct for the protection of others against harm.

2. There has to be a failure to conform to those standards, some breach of duty. The consequences of the failure have to be foreseeable.

3. A connection has to be established by which the harm can be said to be the result of the failure to conform to the established standards. This connection is usually called "proximate cause."

4. It must be established that actual loss or harm to the person or property of another occurred.

The failure to conform to standards in and of itself is not tortious. The failure must be in regard to a person who was owed the duty of care. This point will be elucidated in the next section.

The question of proximate cause is complex. The cases speak of proximate cause as that which, in a natural and continuous sequence, unbroken by any efficient intervening cause, produces the injury, and without which the result would not have occurred.[1] This seems simple, but consider that the cause in fact is not necessarily the proximate cause. When a person slips on a banana peel in the library, the cause in fact is the banana peel; the person who dropped it is perhaps morally reprehensible, but the proximate cause, if there is negligence, is the failure on the part of the library to find and clean up the peel. Then there is the question of how remote the harm can be from the negligent act or omission either in time or space. A leading case, and the darling of every torts professor, is *Palsgraf v. L.I. Railroad Co.*,[2] a 1928 case in which railroad employees tried to help a passenger to board a crowded train. In the process a package containing fireworks was dislodged from the person's arms and exploded on hitting the track. The explosion somehow tipped over a scales at the far end of the platform injuring Mrs. Palsgraf. If one invokes the "but for" test (but for the negligent act of dislodging the fireworks the scales would not have tipped over and Mrs. Palsgraf would not have been harmed), the act of the railroad workers would seem to be the proximate cause. Not so, said the New York Court of Appeals, the state's highest court. Mrs. Palsgraf was simply too far removed from the circle of people that the railroad workers had a duty to protect and thus they were not negligent toward her. Suppose she and the scales had been halfway down the platform: What then?

Foreseeability might seem a problem in the Palsgraf case, but in fact what is contemplated in the term is the reasonable anticipation that harm or injury is a likely result of acts or omissions. One does not have to foresee the very injury that actually occurred to the victim. Indeed, over the years the courts have found foreseeable some of the unlikeliest of consequences.

The fact, noted in number 4 above, that actual damage must occur before negligence will lie, is fairly simple to explain. One, if there is no victim, who will bring the suit? More important, perhaps, is that without a victim's actions all the pieces are not in place to determine whether there was negligence as a matter of law. The defenses to a negligence claim include the last clear chance doctrine, assumption of risk, and contributory negligence, and without testing these and others one doesn't really know whether there has been negligence or not or who must bear the cost if there is. Presumably, the threat of harm occurring is incentive enough to produce the action that will prevent the harm. It is true, of course, that there are many statutes requiring that certain measures be taken, such as providing fire escapes and gates at railroad crossings. One does not have to wait for harm to be done to find a party in violation of the statute.

What Duty Is Owed—Classifications of Persons Entering the Premises

Over the centuries the law developed levels of duty that depended on such things as the danger involved, and to some extent, the relation existing between the parties involved. For example, people operating public conveyances were held to a very high level of duty, perhaps because the dangers of the stagecoach and later the train were sufficiently great to require the highest duty of care to those who were passengers. Perhaps, in part at least, the highest duty of care derived from the fact that the operator of a public conveyance held himself out to be especially capable of protecting the public in this area of work, and he was held to that implied level of care. Thus a range of occupations in which people entrusted their well-being to another were expected to provide the highest duty of care. Other occupations and social situations required only an ordinary duty of care while other situations demanded only that one should not go out of his or her way to cause harm to others. To a large extent, these levels of duty of care have been superseded by the concept applicable in all situations that the duty of care required is that which a reasonably prudent person would do in the circumstances. This would seem a much more reasonable approach than the mechanistic application of levels of duty to certain occupations, but in fact only the words have changed; for example, where in the past people working with high explosives were expected to provide the highest duty of care because of the danger involved, the reasonably prudent person today would also be expected to provide the highest duty of care because that person would recognize the danger involved.

While generally the levels of duty owed have been recast into what the reasonably prudent person would do in the circumstances, there remain classifications of persons' relation to the premises that further determine the duty owed to that person. The classifications are trespasser, licensee, and invitee. Stemming from the late Middle Ages, these concepts reflect the notion that one's status was determined by his or her relation to the land. What that relation was determined what level of care was owed to the individual who came on the premises. That principle holds true today in the majority of the states in this country and applies to any person who may come into the library and be harmed.

It should be very clear that the classifications of people on the premises relate only to defenses when some harm has come to one on the premises. It would be foolhardy to plan operations on the theory that, for the most part, only a minimal or perhaps no duty of care would exist.

Trespassers

A trespasser is any person who is on the premises without permission or without some right to be there. With libraries open to the public, it might seem that nobody could qualify as a trespasser, but that is not true. Anyone in the library when the library is closed and not involved in some sanctioned business with the library would probably be a trespasser. Anyone in areas of the library not open to the public who is not engaged in some recognized business with the library might be a trespasser.

The ancient rule was that the trespasser commanded no right to any care. He took the land or premises as he found them, and if harm befell him that was his problem. This rather harsh approach has been modified over the years in various ways but it is still true that an unknown trespasser has few rights. Thus, if someone should enter the library to escape the cold after closing hours and while there slip on a banana peel, that person could not hope to sue the library for negligence. However, if people constantly cut through the library's parking lot as a shortcut, the library may have, assuming heroic measures have not been taken to deter such passage, an obligation at least to warn such trespassers of any life-threatening artificial, that is, man-made (but not natural), dangers that may not be obvious.

As noted, a trespasser of whom the library is unaware is owed little duty of care. However, once the presence of the trespasser becomes known, there is an obligation of care in the use of dangerous or hazardous materials or machinery. And there will be a duty to warn of dangerous (again artificial) conditions that are not obvious. Of course, the whole building is man-made and thus artificial in the eyes of the law.

The next question is what duty would the library have to assist a known trespasser if harm has come to him? The older cases held that if the harm was not caused by some failure of duty on the part of the land owner, there was no duty to assist him. Obviously, if the harm was caused by some breach of duty there is an affirmative duty to render assistance. In connection with the person injured on the premises, some courts in the last few decades have found a duty to give aid. On the other hand, injuries to a trespasser inflicted by a third party would not impose a legal duty to provide assistance. Absent a special relationship, the law does not require us to be our brother's keeper. One case, the name of which is now forgotten, involved two persons, one of whom taunted the other into jumping into a swimming pool, and then stood idly by as the person drowned. No negligence was found because the possible rescuer had no duty toward the drowning person. Should a trespasser be struck and left bleeding in the library's parking lot, it is probable that much of the staff would rush out to help the person, but there is no obligation to do so. Indeed, if the aid is given in a negligent manner that would be grounds for a suit where none would lie if no aid were given.

Every trespasser has the right to be free of willful or wanton misconduct on the part of the owner or possessor of the land. This is a somewhat elusive concept, but implied is a high degree of recklessness toward the safety of others. "Willful" means intentional, but the concept does not require actual intent to do harm, but rather simply to have such a disregard for the safety of others as to rise nearly to the level of intentionally inflicting harm on another. There is, of course, a right to eject a trespasser by use of reasonable force. Reasonable force means enough force to carry the trespasser off the premises but it does not include inflicting grievous bodily harm or causing death. If, in the course of ejection, the owner has real fear for his own life or of grievous bodily harm, he would then have the right to use deadly force. Of course, the better course of action would be to call the police.

Licensees

A licensee is generally defined as one who is merely allowed to be on the premises but whose purpose for being there is to his benefit only. An example would be a person allowed, either expressly or impliedly, to take a shortcut across the grounds. Only two things need to be looked at to determine the status of licensee: permission and the purpose for being on the premises.

Express permission to be on the premises offers no problem as long as the person granting the permission has the right to do so. Implied permission can raise problems, but generally such things as failure to object, or the maintenance of a pathway or roadway, or the placement of benches or a drinking fountain might suggest that the public was allowed to use the premises.

Certain groups have been held, as a matter of law, to be licensees regardless of the actual facts surrounding their presence on the premises. Included here are canvassers and solicitors, persons seeking shelter from a storm, and social guests.

The question of purpose for being on the premises asks whether the person is there for his purpose only or also for the benefit, traditionally understood as economic benefit, of the owner. If there is economic benefit to the owner then the person is classified as an invitee, which carries the highest duty of care. The classification of invitee evidently developed with the shopkeeper in mind. The obvious problem of thinking in purely economic terms is that for many institutions direct economic benefit cannot be found, yet the institution is doing the business it is designed to do. The library is a perfect example of this. This will be discussed further in the section on invitees below.

In earlier times the rule was that licensees deserved no greater duty of care than did a trespasser. The modern rule, generally followed by American courts, requires the landowner to warn licensees of any unreasonably dangerous hidden conditions, both artificial and natural, not known to the licensee, to exercise reasonable care to make conditions safe, and to exercise reasonable care not actively to harm the licensee. Thus the licensee enjoys a higher degree of duty than the *unknown* trespasser, to whom the landowner owes only a duty to refrain from intentionally harmful or willful or wanton conduct. The licensee enjoys a higher degree of care than that owed to the known or constant trespasser also, in that an activity need not be threatening to life and limb before there is a duty to warn, and a landowner must warn of unreasonably dangerous natural as well as artificial conditions. As a general rule, the licensee has the right to know what the owner knows or reasonably ought to know about the condition of the premises. If the danger is hidden there is a duty to warn, but if the danger is open and obvious the licensee has the obligation to look out for himself. Usually, a warning is sufficient to protect the owner from a charge of negligence.

Invitees

An invitee is a person who enters the premises for the benefit of the owner or for the mutual benefit of the owner and the entrant. As noted above, this benefit was traditionally interpreted as an economic benefit, which caused several problems. Not only are there many institutions at which no monetary transactions take place, but there was the question of how to classify such people as delivery men who entered for their own economic benefit yet whose entrance was a necessary part of the owner's business activity. What of the child who accompanies its mother to the store? Clearly the traditional approach was deficient.

Several decades ago the late Dean Prosser suggested a new approach to the invitee status,[3] one that has been uniformly adopted by American courts. The heart of the matter, he said, was not the economic benefit conferred but rather the implied safety and suitability of the premises for the purpose for which an invitation to enter is held out. An invitation to enter can be said to apply to any of the numerous ways businesses and institutions inform the public that its presence is welcome. Anyone who enters with the aim of transacting the business of that entity does so as an invitee.

It can be seen, of course, that this approach still does not meet all the problems. That child with its mother is not there to transact any business, the person saying good-bye to a passenger at the train station isn't doing any business with the railroad, yet courts will uniformly find these people to be invitees. The presence of these people indirectly furthers the business at hand and this is evidently sufficient.

It follows that the duty of care owed to invitees is very high. Quite naturally the duty owed includes all the duty owed to trespassers and licensees. Again, as with licensees, the entrant is owed reasonable care in warning about dangerous conditions, but as the duty of care is higher, the diligence required to discover hazardous conditions will be greater. Reasonable care to an invitee is at a higher level than reasonable care to a licensee. Thus an act of reasonable care to a licensee might be a bar to negligence, whereas the very same act toward an invitee would be insufficient. Further, since the invitee enters with the expectation that the premises are safe, he is not under the same obligation as a licensee to look out for his own safety. It is therefore incumbent upon the owner to take greater steps to insure the safety of the invitee, including correction of the dangerous condition.

The duty to an invitee does not extend to all possible dangers but only to those that are unreasonably dangerous. A flight of stairs, for instance, is dangerous and accidents do happen on them. But the danger is open and obvious and the user is able to assess whether the climb is worth the risk. No special care with regard to an ordinary flight of stairs is required. On the other hand, if one of the treads is missing, the likelihood of this being discovered by the user (before it's too late) is not assured, but the possibility of harm is great; thus the condition would be unreasonably dangerous and some action by the owner would be required.

Abolition of the Categories

Apparently taking the view that the categories were overly protective of property interests, the California Supreme Court in the 1968 case of *Roland v. Christian*[4] abolished the distinctions made by the three categories. In the following ten years or so another eight states, either by the court or in the legislature, abolished the categories although Colorado, whose court had removed the categories, attempted (ineptly) to reestablish them by statute in 1986 and finally got the job done in 1990.[5] In the same time period another five states abolished the distinction between licensee and invitee but retained the category of trespasser. In the 1980s three more states had adopted this last approach. Ten years ago commentators on the matter assumed all states would jump on the abolition bandwagon, but positions seem to have hardened and those thirty-four states that have retained the categories evidently will continue to do so.

The following states have, to date, abolished the categories: Alaska, California, Hawaii, Louisiana, Missouri, New Hampshire, New York, and Rhode Island. The states that have abolished the distinction between licensee and invitee but retained trespasser are: Florida, Illinois, Maine, Massachusetts, Minnesota, North Dakota, Tennessee, and Wisconsin. In place of the law that had developed around the categories, the above states introduced ordinary negligence principles of foreseeable risk and reasonable care.

Any library is likely, if the library is in a state that recognizes categories, to encounter entrants representing all three categories, but most will be invitees and some might be licensees. Since the distinction between licensee and invitee turns on whether the entrant is there for his own benefit or is engaged in the business of the entity, it behooves the library to state very clearly what its business is and what it is not. Generally speaking, the library's function is to provide information; in the process, most libraries open to the public maintain rest rooms, copying machines, and public telephones. Clearly, a patron who enters the library to do some research is an invitee and does not lose that status if at some point he takes time out to make a phone call unrelated to the research. If, however, an individual comes into the library solely to make a personal phone call, that person would properly be a licensee if the library has made clear to the public what the invitation into the building was for: that is, to gather information, not merely to make use of various conveniences. It might save the library or the community or the institution of which the library is a part some money. This is not to suggest, however, that a library would necessarily be wrong in viewing the provision of such services as an integral part of the services the library supplies. This is clearly a policy decision, albeit one affected by the licensee/invitee dichotomy.

Governmental Immunities

As many libraries are governmental agencies, some consideration of governmental immunities must be included in this discussion, although it is a matter of far less concern than it was twenty or more years ago. Centuries ago the concept that the king could do no wrong was developed and generally called sovereign immunity. Various legal theories have been put forward to support the concept, although none are particularly persuasive. Regardless of its theoretical underpinnings, sovereign immunity served for many years to insulate the government and its agencies from tort actions. Perhaps recognizing the essential unfairness of the doctrine—after all, it hurts just as much when the postal person negligently runs over your child as when your neighbor does—governments at all levels have been abandoning the immunity.

In 1946 the federal government passed the Federal Tort Claims Act (FTCA). The act provided that the federal government could be sued for any negligent or wrongful act or omission perpetrated by a government employee in the course of carrying out his duties under circumstances where the United States, if a private person, would be liable to the claimant in accordance with the law of the place where the act or omission took place.

As the number of federal libraries is small in the totality of libraries, discussion of FTCA will be limited to mentioning its existence, except to note that there are a number of exclusions in the act. Perhaps the most important exclusion is that which prohibits suits based on discretionary actions of governmental officials. Many suits have been generated over the question of what is discretionary and what is ministerial. The courts generally find that the running of buildings is ministerial and thus the negligent actions or omissions in a federal library would be open to suit under FTCA.

Most states have taken some steps to abrogate their sovereign immunity, but it is extremely difficult to generalize. Some states have given up their immunity but created exceptions. Texas, for example, will allow itself to be sued in tort but has stipulated that entrants onto state land are to be classed as licensees unless they have paid for the entrance. Other states have abandoned the immunity but have placed limits on the amount of recovery allowed. And even this has been refined. Rhode Island allows complete recovery if the negligence is caused by a proprietary agency of the government, but puts a limit of $100,000 for recovery against negligent acts or omissions made by a governmental agency in carrying out its agency duties.

The law of governmental immunities has long recognized the distinction between governmental and proprietary activities. Some are obvious: for example, a municipal water supply that sells water to its customers is clearly engaged in a proprietary activity. The operation of schools is purely a governmental activity. Problems arise with activities such as public parks or swimming pools, especially if they charge admission. So distinctions can be difficult, but where governmental immunity exists, the distinctions can be crucial. The rule is, in those jurisdictions that recognize the immunity, governmental activities are accorded immunity while proprietary activities are not.

The distinction between discretionary and ministerial acts alluded to in the above discussion of federal claims exists at all levels of government. The rule that the FTCA embraced is merely a statement of the traditional and accepted approach in immunity law. That is, discretionary acts or omissions are immune from suit while ministerial acts or omissions are not.

The library administrator should determine where his or her state stands on sovereign immunity, and if it exists, determine whether the library's particular activity is governmental or proprietary. As schools are governmental, it follows that school libraries and, perhaps, public university libraries would enjoy governmental immunity. Public libraries are questionable, and, like public parks, it could be argued that they may be either governmental or proprietary.   Finally, it should be noted that governmental immunity protects against ordinary negligence; willful and wanton behavior will uniformly remove the shield of governmental immunity.

Charitable Immunities

Charitable immunity works to shield charitable institutions, just as governmental immunity shields the government.   However, it is a concept that has been abandoned nearly everywhere and requires only the comment here that if your library is part of a charitable organization such as a hospital, it might be worthwhile to examine the status of the immunity in your state.

Other Defenses
Contributory Negligence

Contributory negligence is a concept in which the person harmed contributed some element of fault in being harmed. The legal theory is that the harmed person's fault combines with the fault of the other party to form the proximate cause. It is an element without which there would have been no injury. The concept doesn't look to see if the contributed fault is very great, only if it is there at all. And if it is found, the result is that the harmed person cannot recover. This is fair enough if both parties are equally at fault, but clearly too harsh if the victim is only slightly responsible for the injury and the other party overwhelmingly so. By 1988 only six states followed the rule of contributory negligence: Alabama, Maryland, North Carolina, South Carolina, Tennessee, and Virginia, and also the District of Columbia. It can be a powerful defense if you happen to be in one of those jurisdictions.

Last Clear Chance Doctrine

The last clear chance doctrine was a device by which courts attempted to mitigate the harshness of contributory negligence. It comes into play where the victim has been negligent, to some degree, and yet the defendant could have avoided causing or inflicting the injury. The underlying theories of the operation of this doctrine are many and muddled. The result, however, is that the defendant's negligence becomes the proximate cause of the harm, and the victim is absolved of his negligence and can recover for his injuries. As few states now recognize contributory negligence, the importance of the doctrine is far less than it once was.

Comparative Negligence

Contributory negligence puts the entire burden of loss on the victim if the victim has been negligent. The last clear chance doctrine shifts the entire burden of loss to the defendant. Neither approach takes into account the amount of negligence each party contributed to the harm done. In the past twenty-five years most states, either judicially or statutorily, have adopted some form of comparative negligence. While there are several variations, the majority of states follow what is known as "pure comparative negligence." Here the victim who has sued the other party for negligence can receive damages reduced by the percentage to which he contributed to the harm. Equitable in theory, the determination of the proper percentage of fault can be difficult.

Assumption of Risk

This doctrine allows one party to assume the risk of any particular activity or, put another way, relieves one party of the duty of care that otherwise would exist. The arrangement can be either expressed or implied. There generally is no public policy against one party signing a waiver absolving another from any duty he might have toward the first party. Someone going to a hockey game impliedly assumes the risk of flying pucks, and players are under no obligation to take particular precautions to protect the attendee. The basis of assumption of risk is that the individual knows that some danger exists but that the desired result is worth running the risk—a decision the individual has a right to make although there is no requirement that the other party must accede. Your neighbor may be willing to assume the risk of petting your vicious dog but you do not have to allow him or her to do it.

Liability in Failure to Protect Against Acts of Third Parties

Harmful acts of third parties, whether intentional, negligent, or criminal, may be attributed to the owner of the premises on which they take place. At first blush this may seem unfair, because, as the owner can't control the actions of the third party, the owner should be held innocent of that party's actions. It would seem to be a wholly different situation when, instead of the owner harming an entrant, there is one entrant harming another entrant. Surely the argument must be between those two, and indeed it is. If A and B are both invitees in the library and A harms B, B may well be able to sue A for the harm. The question is, can B also sue the library? The answer lies in an examination of the issues common to any negligence cause of action: establishing the existence and breach of a duty, foreseeability, and causation.

Undoubtedly, the library owes a duty to B, and it would appear that that duty has been breached if she has been harmed. Foreseeability and causation would clearly be difficult obstacles for B to overcome, but the situation may allow that to happen.

With foreseeability the question would be whether the library knew or should have known that A would do what he did. A's own previous actions might have made the present action foreseeable. Let's say that A punched B. If A had punched several other women in the past week, and been caught, the library should have known that A was likely to do it again and taken appropriate action to prevent it. Past incidents not involving A might also make a deed foreseeable. If the library had a poorly lit, hidden area in the stacks where rapes had taken place previously and A raped B in that spot, that rape could be found to be foreseeable. In fact, the previous crimes would not necessarily have to be the same, but they would have to be of a similar nature. Thus, assaults or handbag snatching in the area would establish the area as dangerous to one's person; the fact that this dim, hidden area was the frequent scene of copyright infringement alone would not do.

The matter of causation is the usual one: Did the library's act or omission cause or allow the harm to happen? That is, was this the proximate cause? It should be obvious that the act or omission must reasonably be the cause of the harm, and that, had the right thing been done, the harm would not have occurred. A roller skate on the top step cannot be the proximate cause of a fall by a person falling anywhere but at the top step. One man who hit a train sued the railroad for failure to have a crossing gate. The court, noting that the man ran into the sixty-eighth car of the train, felt that the presence of the proper gate would not have averted the accident and thus the absence of a gate was not a proximate cause.

In short, a library, like any owner, is responsible for the safety and well-being of invitees, and the fact that the harm comes from a third party rather than a library employee or a physical object in the library may have no bearing. The third party is just like any other thing that can cause harm, and the library has the responsibility to take corrective action if it knows or should know either that a particular third party is dangerous, or that a condition exists conducive to harmful activity by third parties.

Liability for Some Intentional Torts

Librarians are not in the habit of intentionally causing people harm, but in the area of protecting property they may easily commit a number of torts. In

protecting property it is impermissible to use devices that would produce grievous bodily harm or death. Unlikely as it may be that librarians would resort to
such measures, be forewarned that the use of spring guns, traps, land mines, or
any other such device used to protect property will not be countenanced in the
law. The rule is that you may not use greater force in absentia than you could
use if you were present. The results of such cases are nearly uniform: the bur-
glar trips the wire to the spring gun, is wounded, successfully sues his intended
victim and, though perhaps limping, lives a life of ease on the proceeds of the
suit. No such case has been found in a library context to date, however.

Instrumentalities that could inflict some harm but are not threatening to
life or limb are permissible if they are reasonably necessary to protect the possession. Thus, barbed wire could be used to protect a lumber yard. Whether
it would be reasonable to use it around the library's parking lot is somewhat
questionable. Hidden devices that can cause some harm are not permissible
unless there is adequate warning that would seem to take away some of the
purpose in hiding the device. All is not foolish, however. A trained guard dog
prowling the premises might be considered a hidden device, and yet a warning probably enhances rather than negates his effectiveness.

It is in the area of actually apprehending thieves, however, that the librarian
runs the greatest risk of committing a tort. While librarians have the undeniable right to stop anyone from taking material belonging to the library, the question arises in the execution. Take a situation where a staffer thinks a patron has
concealed an item belonging to the library. The patron is in the process of leaving the building without checking out the item. What does the staffer do? Typically, he will ask the patron if he has remembered to check out all library items.
Suppose the patron states there is nothing to check out, and suppose further
that the item thought to be concealed is one of great value. At this point the staff
member has a choice: to let the patron go whether believing him or not, or to
detain him in order to search for the concealed item. The patron thinks it's
time to leave and heads for the exit. The staffer shouts, "Stop that thief!"
whereupon two burly library aides appear and grab the patron, holding him
against his will. The patron is then held until the police can arrive to conduct a
search of the person for the concealed item. If a concealed item is found,
everything is fine; if not, however, there are serious problems facing the library.

Certainly there is the right of citizen's arrest, and certainly one has the
right to detain thieves for the purpose of regaining one's property. The problem is that in detaining another, whether as a citizen's arrest or merely to
regain one's property, the person doing the detaining must be right. No matter how reasonable the belief that a thief has been nabbed, the nabber is open
to suit if, in fact, he is wrong.

In the library situation outlined above, if no concealed item is turned up,
the library is open to four separate torts. First, in calling out "Stop that thief!"

the library has slandered the individual as long as there was a third person to hear the statement. And evidently there was, in the persons of the library aides who apprehended the patron. In the apprehension, the patron may have been menaced, which may constitute assault, and if the aids physically restrained the patron, that is a battery. Finally, in holding the patron against his will, the library has committed the tort of false imprisonment. These torts are serious because our society places great value both on the unsullied character of one's person and on one's freedom. The lesson to be learned is that one must be not only positive but in fact right that a theft has taken place before one impedes the egress of a patron.

Most states have shoplifter statutes that allow shop owners to detain, for a reasonable time, persons suspected of stealing, during which the police are summoned. The statutes absolve the shopkeeper from all tort liability if he acted reasonably, even if he or she was mistaken. In most cases the statutes are so worded that they apply to commercial establishments only, and libraries would not be shielded if they erroneously detained a suspected thief. Some states have statutes that apply the shoplifter statute principles specifically to libraries, and in other states the shoplifter laws are written broadly to cover other institutions as well as retail stores. All libraries should check the status of their protection under such statutes, and if such coverage is lacking, work toward passage of appropriate legislation.

Conclusion

The responsibility one has to another is, in the eyes of the law, a fairly complex matter, as the foregoing has perhaps suggested. Clearly, one should conduct oneself, whether as an individual or as a library administrator, in accordance with the law. On the other hand, there are ethical and moral questions in basing one's conduct purely on the dictates of the law. What thinking person would feel easy in ignoring a crying baby abandoned in a snowbank simply because the law said there was no duty to that child? On the other hand, knowing the law allows one to concentrate resources where they are most needed. Knowing, for example, that trespassers are owed practically no duty of care allows the library to turn its lights off at night. This is useful, and when sued it is useful to know that damages may be limited by application of law. On the other hand, the overriding concern should be for the safety of one's fellow creatures: the guiding principle ought to be, Do the right thing. Librarians should take heart in the fact that, in preparation for this paper, a computer search turned up very few cases involving libraries. Librarians must be doing the right thing. The majority of cases that did turn up seemed to involve bookmobiles. Beware of bookmobiles.

NOTES

1. Swayne v. Connecticut Co., 86 Conn. 439 (1913).

2. 248 N.Y. 339 (1928).

3. William D. Prosser, "Business Visitors and Invitees," *Minnesota Law Review* 26:573–612 (1942).

4. 70 Cal. Rptr. 97 (1989).

5. See Gallegos v. Phipps, 779 P.2d 856 (1989).

2

DISCRIMINATION IN EMPLOYMENT

One of the finest ideals of the American ethos is that all men are created equal. One can safely assume that Jefferson meant all persons, and was not leaving out women and children. Current sensitivity to language calls for recognition of that fact. It was and remains a self-evident truth, but unfortunately true equality continues to be an elusive goal. Both federal and state governments have, over the years, attempted to redress the problem through legislation, and with a number of favorable Supreme Court decisions, much progress has been made. For instance, policies discriminatory to a minority race are never constitutional. It is undeniable, however, that there are still identifiable groups without protection from discrimination and it is certainly true that many minority groups and women continue to endure inequities to a greater or lesser degree economically, socially, and culturally.

The purpose of this chapter is to analyze those legislative acts designed to affect discriminatory practices for their impact on libraries and librarians. Librarians as employers are probably among the most sensitive of the rights of others, and instances of discrimination in the library workplace are few if the paucity of court cases is any measure. Still, the requirements of any employer under the various pieces of legislation are not always obvious, and therefore it should be useful to see what the requirements are. Employees, of course, should also be interested in knowing what rights they have. While much of the legislation is directed at discrimination in employment, there is legislation against other types of discrimination, such as in access to public buildings by the disabled, and these too will be analyzed.

There are four major acts on the federal level protecting persons against discrimination in employment: the Equal Pay Act (EPA) (1963), Title VII of the Civil Rights Act (1964), the Age Discrimination in Employment Act (ADEA) (1967), and the Americans with Disabilities Act (ADA) (1990). The Rehabilitation Act of 1973 (RA) remains a major piece of legislation with regard to the federal government and those with federal contracts or receiving federal funds. The ADA has, to a large degree, incorporated the RA's definitions and implementation procedures; therefore, detailed discussion of the RA is not included. The Civil Rights Act of 1991 incorporates a number of amendments to the acts noted above. The thrust of the Civil Rights Act of 1991 is to reverse Supreme Court decisions of the late 1980s which Congress felt misinterpreted the several acts in various ways. The provisions of the 1991 act will be discussed at the appropriate point rather than separately.

The Equal Pay Act of 1963

The Equal Pay Act (EPA or the Act) was signed into law July 10, 1963, as an amendment to the Fair Labor Standards Act (FLSA) (29 USC 206(d)). The Act is designed to combat unequal pay between the sexes for equal work. Its focus is very narrow and covers only discrimination concerning unequal pay, and only where that discrimination is on the basis of sex. Either sex is protected, although the overwhelming number of cases involve women who are paid less than men for doing the same work. Initially, regulation and enforcement of the Act were by the U.S. Department of Labor, but in 1978 responsibility for the Act was assigned to the Equal Employment Opportunities Commission (EEOC), which rewrote the regulations in 1986 (29 CFR 1620).

The Act is breathtakingly brief, being less than one page, and the substantive portion a single paragraph that reads in its entirety:

> No employer having employees subject to any provisions of this section shall discriminate, within any establishment in which such employees are employed, between employees on the basis of sex by paying wages to employees in such establishment at a rate less than the rate at which he pays wages to employees of the opposite sex in such establishment for equal work on jobs the performance of which requires equal skill, effort, and responsibility, and which are performed under similar working conditions, except where such payment is made pursuant to (i) a seniority system; (ii) a merit system; (iii) a system which measures earnings by quantity or quality of production; or (iv) a differential based on any other factor other than sex: Provided, That an employer who is paying a wage rate differential in violation of the subsection shall not, in order to comply with the provisions of this subsection, reduce the wage rate of any employee.
> (29 USCS s206(d)(1))

Although brief, these few words do require some explication, which is informed by the regulations and court cases.

Coverage

Since the Equal Pay Act is a part of the Fair Labor Standards Act, it has the same basic coverage as the FLSA, which is extremely broad. The regulations provide coverage for employees "engaged in commerce" or "engaged in the production of goods for commerce." This doesn't sound like the stuff of libraries, but in fact libraries do order materials that travel in interstate commerce and they do generate information and materials, which is the production of goods as the Act interprets that term. Coverage is not based on the amount or percentage of work in which the employee is engaged in commerce or in the production of goods for commerce, although the work ought to be on a regular and recurring basis. Coverage goes to the individual so engaged but also covered are those individuals whose work is so closely related to such commerce as to be considered a part of it. Thus, a reference librarian calling up information online from an out-of-state database is clearly engaged in commerce, but the systems expert who set up the computer configuration to allow the online search is undoubtedly also engaged in commerce.

The Act also recognizes "enterprise" coverage. Under the enterprise concept, if an entity is an enterprise engaged in commerce or in the production of goods for commerce, every employee of such enterprise is covered by the Equal Protection Act unless specifically exempted by the FLSA. There are two ways in which an entity can achieve enterprise status. One is to belong in one of the four designated categories:

a. Public agencies. Coverage here extends to federal, state, and local governmental entities including, of course, public libraries.

b. Schools and hospitals. All schools regardless of level, whether charitable or for profit, are included as are all hospitals, charitable or for profit, regardless of type of care given.

c. Laundries. Seemingly a bit incongruous with the other designated enterprises, this category includes anything that remotely looks like a laundry: dry cleaning establishments, linen supply companies, coin operated laundromats, even carpet cleaning companies.

d. Construction. This category includes any entity involved in any of the building trades or remotely related thereto. The obvious categories are carpentry, bricklaying, plumbing, and the like, but also included are landscaping and perhaps interior decorating.

The other way to earn enterprise status is to do a certain dollar volume of business. If the enterprise is a nonretail establishment, the sales made or business done must reach $250,000 per year, or, if in the business of retail sales or service, the annual dollar volume must reach $362,500. In addition, there must be a minimal employee contact with commerce, which can be satisfied by having two or more employees covered by traditional concepts, that is, "engaged in commerce" or "engaged in production of goods for commerce."

The Equal Pay Act applies to executive, administrative, and professional employees who are normally exempted from the FLSA. The Act also covers all state and local government employees unless specifically exempted.

Equal Work

The focus of the Act is on the question of whether individuals of opposite sexes are performing equal work for unequal pay. The determination of whether work is equal is somewhat imprecise, but the regulations and the courts are in agreement that the work does not need to be identical, but rather substantially alike in terms of equal skill, effort, and responsibility demanded in performance, and performed under similar working conditions.

Skill

Jobs to which the equal pay is applicable are jobs that require equal skill in their performance. Skill is defined to include experience, training, education, and ability, and must be measured in terms of the performance requirements of the job. The question is not whether the required skills are exercised more often in one job than another, but whether the job requires similar skills. Presumably a brain surgeon who operates once a week needs essentially the same skills as a surgeon who operates daily. As with equal work, equal skills means substantially equal. For example, the courts have found male hospital orderlies and female practical nurses to have jobs requiring substantially equal skills and thus meet the requirements of the Act. However, possession of a skill not needed to meet the requirements of a job cannot be considered in making a determination regarding equality of skill.

Equal Effort

The second element in the determination of equal work is that of equal effort. The measure of effort encompasses both physical and mental activity. Obviously, if the two jobs in question require exactly the same tasks, the effort expended will be equal. However, the Act requires only substantial similarity in the work done, and thus an assessment must be made as to whether the somewhat different jobs require equal effort. For example, a man and a woman may both work at the circulation desk charging out books for eighty percent of the time; in the other twenty percent the man shelves books while the woman files cards into the catalog. Shelving books may require more physical exertion but filing cards requires mental exertion in recognizing not only the alphabetic arrangement but the difference between title and subject cards. While the calories expended may not be the same, it can be assumed that the tasks require similar efforts, and therefore fulfill that part of the Act requiring equal effort.

If a job entails extra duties those duties must be substantial to qualify for a differential in pay. If they are substantial, the jobs aren't equal, but some insignificant task such as turning out the lights does not measure up. In any event, the extra duties themselves must be paid at an amount commensurate with pay accorded to members of the opposite sex for performance of the same tasks.

Equal Responsibility

The equal pay standard applies to jobs whose performance requires equal responsibility. Responsibility is concerned with the degree of accountability required in the performance of the job, which is usually determined in economic or social terms. For instance, two library clerks, one male and one female, whose jobs are similar in approving applications for library use, could be paid at a different rate if one approved applications for use of the general collection and the other was responsible for approving the use of rare books. The mere fact that one individual is held responsible for a particular performance is sufficient reason for a pay differential. For example, if reference librarians Smith and Jones equally share the task for actually turning off lights and securing the building at closing but librarian Smith bears the blame if the closing isn't done properly, there is a basis for a differential in pay.

Similar Working Conditions

In order for the equal pay standard to apply, the jobs must be performed under similar working conditions. The term "similar working conditions" encompasses two subfactors: "surroundings," which measures the intensity and frequency of such elements as toxic chemicals or fumes regularly encountered by workers, and "hazards," which takes into account physical dangers regularly encountered, their frequency, and the severity of injury they can cause. One court has said these are the only factors to be used in determining similarity of working conditions,[1] but the EEOC regulations state that in determining whether the requirement is met, a practical judgment is mandatory in light of whether the differences in working conditions are the kind customarily taken into consideration in setting wage levels (29 CFR 1620.18 (a)).

Defenses

Once a differential in pay for equal work has been established, the burden shifts to the defendant to establish a defense based on one of the four defenses listed in the Act: seniority, merit, a system that measures earnings by quantity or quality of production, or factors other than sex.

Seniority

Seniority is a valid defense if the system is gender neutral and is evenly applied to both sexes. The Act uses the term "seniority system," but this need not be a formalized, written arrangement, and it should be a rational scheme that rewards longevity with increases in pay.

Merit

Merit can be a highly subjective evaluation of a worker's effectiveness, and in order to constitute a valid defense, an employer must be able to prove that the higher-paid individual does in fact have greater merit. This is best done by having a sound evaluation process based as much as possible on objective factors. Any merit system that over a period of time rates one sex consistently higher than the other will be suspect.

Quantity and Quality of Production

The proviso making quantity and quality of production a defense actually adds little. Any system that pays by quantity of production will have a wage rate by which the quantity is rewarded. Obviously, the wage rate must not discriminate between the sexes, but the application of the wage rate can and probably will result in a difference in pay earned depending on which person produces more. Evaluation of the quality of production is really no different from evaluating merit.

Factors Other Than Sex

"Factors other than sex" is a catchall category in which the employer must put forward a rational reason, other than sex, why there is a differential in pay for equal jobs. It must be noted at the outset that market conditions in which one gender is willing to work for less is not a "factor other than sex." This, indeed, is the heart of the matter the Act is designed to remedy. Premium pay for heads of households is generally not a factor other than sex, and the EEOC states that such a claimed defense will be scrutinized closely. Likewise, a claim that costs of employment of one sex require a differential in pay will not be recognized as a factor other than sex.

Red Circle Rates

The regulations specifically recognize so-called "red circle" rates as a factor other than sex. The term "red circle" rate is used to describe a temporarily higher wage rate for a job than the job normally receives. A typical example would be where a skilled, higher-paid individual is asked, for the same higher pay, temporarily to perform a lower paying job in which a member of the opposite sex is performing the job at the lower wage. Similarly, a lower-paid person may temporarily be assigned a higher paying job without raising his or her pay to the level paid a member of the opposite sex performing equal work. As long as these reassignments are temporary, the pay differential will be excused as resulting from a factor other than sex. The regulations see one month as the limit of a temporary assignment.

Other Examples of Factors Other Than Sex

1. Training programs. An individual in a valid training program can be paid a premium while performing equal work with lower-paid members of the opposite sex. However, the program must be bona fide, as evidenced by such things as a regular rotation through departments, training sessions, a plan of progression, an expectation of promotion, and gender neutrality. It would help the defense if the employer affirmatively sought members of both sexes for the program.

2. Level of education. A higher level of training or education can be a factor other than sex permitting a differential in pay, if there is a rational connection between the education and the job. This would seem to be a slim reed on which to defend without more. The mere expectation that greater education will provide better performance without realization of such performance should not be a defense. If there is realization of better performance, the Act provides the defenses of either merit or quality of production to justify a differential in pay. If job performance is equal despite the added education, it would seem only fair that the pay be equal too. There are, however, some jobs where it is difficult to discern the effect of added education.

3. Temporary and part-time positions. Under the regulations promulgated by the Department of Labor,[2] employers may pay their permanent staff at a different rate from temporary and part-time positions if it can be shown that economic considerations require a differential in order to attract less than full-time help. However, the superseding regulations issued by the EEOC in 1986 do not include this provision.

4. Shift differential. Paying a premium for work on a less desirable shift is a factor other than sex and is allowable provided that the shift commanding a premium is open equally to persons of both sexes.[3]

5. Flexibility of employees. Where employees of both sexes do essentially equal work but where one employee possesses an extra ability to provide a special usefulness to the employer, that flexibility may be a legitimate factor other than sex for a differential in pay. There are few cases on this particular point, and one can't be sure how far this point can be taken. In *Marshall v. St. John Valley Security Home*,[4] the court found that male ambulance drivers, who ninety-eight percent of the time performed duties similar to female nurse's

aides, did not perform the same work, for while ambulance duty was less than two percent of the job, the essence of an attendant's job is to be on call to discharge ambulance duties, which require a higher degree of skill, effort, and responsibility. It is doubtful that a male circulation desk clerk with a knowledge of Sanskrit could be paid more than a female counterpart, for the essence of his job is not to be ready to translate Sanskrit but to conduct circulation business. On the other hand, if that male possessed a competence in reprogramming the computers that are vital to the circulation process and such reprogramming is occasionally required, that person could be paid more than his female counterpart providing she does not have that skill. However, if the library has computer people able to fix any malfunction in the circulation computer available, the possession of the skill by the desk clerk is no longer essential and one could not argue that the essence of the clerk's job was to be on call to fix the computer. Disparity in pay for that would seem discriminatory unless a valid claim can be made that the pay differential is based on the actual accomplishment of extra duties that are sufficient to satisfy the Act and regulations.

Remedies and Procedures

Where one sex is paid a higher wage rate than the other for the performance of equal work, the higher rate serves as the wage standard. When a violation of the Equal Protection Act is established, the higher rate paid is the standard to which the lower rate paid must be raised to remedy the violation. Under the express terms of the Act an employer may not correct a sex-based differential by lowering the wages of the higher paid sex, nor may an employer transfer one sex to a different job or to a different establishment.

Enforcement

Suits alleging discrimination under the Act can be initiated by the aggrieved employee or by the government through the EEOC. Should the government bring suit, the right of private action is precluded. There are no particular procedural requirements the employee must follow as there are with other acts, such as filing with some state or federal agency, no exhaustion of remedies, no conciliation, no requirement for permission to sue. The only bar would be the statute of limitations, which states that the action must begin within two years after the cause of action accrues, or three years if the violation was willful.

The cause of action is a continuing one with each payday constituting a new cause of action, so that the commencement of the action must begin within two years of the latest violation or three if the violation is willful. The statute of limitations has the effect of limiting the recovery of back wages to two or three years, as the case may be, prior to the date of the commencement of the action. That date is the date the case is filed with the court.

The question of what is "willful" proved to problematical over the years with the so called "Jiffy June" test,[5] which said that an employer's action was willful if the employer knew the Equal Pay Act was "in the picture." This proved largely to eliminate the two-tier approach as it was virtually impossible for any employer to prove ignorance that the Act might have some bearing on pay policies. In *Transworld Airlines, Inc. v. Thurston*,[6] the Supreme Court adopted a more stringent definition of "willful" as used in the Age Discrimination in Employment Act (ADEA). In that definition the plaintiff had to show "that the employer either knew or showed reckless disregard for the matter of whether its conduct was prohibited by the statute . . ." (at 133). In 1988, the Supreme Court extended this definition to all cases arising under the FLSA, which, of course, includes the Equal Pay Act.[7]

Remedies[8]

An employee who proves discrimination under the Act can secure pay as "back wages" in the amount between what should have been paid and what was actually paid, plus liquidated damages up to an amount equal to the back wages due. An employer can reduce or eliminate liquidated damages by proving that he acted in good faith and had reasonable grounds to believe his pay policy was in compliance with the law. In addition to back pay and liquidated damages, the successful plaintiff is entitled to costs and a reasonable attorney's fee.

The government, by the EEOC, may also bring suit for back pay and liquidated damages and for injunctive relief. The injunctive relief is to enjoin employers from violating the law and from withholding proper compensation. Actions brought under 216(b) and 216(c) of the FLSA are viewed as legal actions affording the plaintiff the right to a jury trial. An action brought for injunctive relief under 217 is equitable in nature and thus does not allow for a jury trial.

The Equal Pay Act and Title VII of the Civil Rights Act of 1964

Title VII prohibits discrimination in all aspects of employment including compensation on various bases including sex. Thus, while Title VII and the Equal Pay Act overlap, they are not coterminous. In situations where the jurisdictional prerequisites of both the EPA and Title VII of the Civil Rights Act are satisfied, any violation of the Equal Pay Act is also a violation of Title VII.

Conversely, any differentiation in pay that is authorized by the EPA will not be discriminatory under Title VII. However, Title VII covers types of wage discrimination not actionable under the EPA. Therefore, an act or practice of an employer not a violation of the EPA because not covered by the EPA may be a violation of Title VII.

Where the discriminatory act is covered by both the EPA and Title VII, recovery may be had under both acts so long as the individual does not receive duplicative relief for the same wrong. Relief for the same individual may be computed under one statute for one or more periods of the violation and under the other statute for other periods of the violation. One would look to those elements of the statute that would provide the greatest relief under the particular circumstances of the individual case. For instance, both acts allow for recovery of back wages for two years prior to filing of the charge, but the EPA allows for liquidated damages while Title VII does not. Title VII, on the other hand, allows for limited compensatory and punitive damages in some circumstances where the EPA does not. A close analysis is necessary to determine the most advantageous route.

Retaliation

Section 15 (A)(3) of the Fair Labor Standards Act forbids reprisals against any employee who asserts his or her rights under the FLSA, and as the Equal Pay Act is structurally a part of FLSA, reprisals under that act are covered as well. Read literally, the section protects only those engaged in proceedings to enforce the act, but in fact the section is given a broad interpretation and protects anyone who even voices an opinion about the Act.

Retaliation includes any act of discrimination against the employee including dismissal, relocation, demotion, or any other deprivation of privileges and benefits because the employee asserted his or her rights under the Act. The section 216 (b)[9] provides the courts with broad powers to rectify the harm done the employee including reinstatement, back wages, promotion, and any other equitable remedy the court may find suitable.

Title VII of the Civil Rights Act of 1964

The Civil Rights Act of 1964 is a very comprehensive enactment covering discrimination in voting rights (Title I), public accommodations and facilities (Titles II and III), education (Title IV), federally assisted programs (Title VI), and employment (Title VII).

It is without doubt that Title VII,[10] Equal Employment Opportunities, has had the greatest impact and engendered the greatest number of lawsuits of any civil rights legislation enacted in the twentieth century. It has also engendered a great deal of political rhetoric and philosophical debate over various aspects of enforcement, such as affirmative action, which gives rise to arguments over "quotas" and "reverse discrimination." Nevertheless, the goals of Title VII are laudatory, the coverage is comprehensive, and the rules are complex; it is an act with which nearly every employer including nearly every library needs be familiar.

The Reach of the Act

Title VII applies to employers, employment agencies, labor organizations, and certain training programs. The definitions of those terms determine whether an entity is covered or not.

1. The term "employer" means a person engaged in an industry affecting commerce who has fifteen or more employees for each working day in each of twenty or more calendar weeks in the current or preceding calendar year. The term does not include the United States or a corporation wholly owned by the government of the United States, Indian tribes, departments of the District of Columbia subject to competitive civil service, and private clubs exempt from taxation under section 501(c) of the Internal Revenue Code.

2. The term "employment agency" means any person regularly undertaking with or without compensation to procure employees for an employer or to procure for employees opportunities to work for an employer. Libraries are certainly not employment agencies but they may use them and thus should know what practices are proscribed. Library schools operating placement offices, however, are employment agencies.

3. Section 2000e defines "labor organization" in detail. Libraries themselves are not likely to be confused with labor organizations, but staff organizations might well meet the criteria defined by the act for a labor organization. Without going into greater detail, suffice it to say that any organization that represents employees' interests against an employer will be a "labor organization" if it has at least fifteen members and in one of several ways is considered to be "engaged in an industry affecting commerce." The easiest way to satisfy this last is the provision that an organization "is an organization recognized or acting as the representative of employees of an employer or employers in an industry affecting commerce."[11]

4. Section 2000e-2(d) makes it unlawful for any employer, labor organization, or joint labor-management committee controlling apprenticeship or other

training or retraining, including on-the-job training programs, to discriminate on the basis of race, color, religion, sex, or national origin in admission to or employment in any program established to provide apprenticeship or other training. The Act does not define apprenticeship programs, and thus assumes the plain-language meaning of "apprenticeship" and "training" programs.

Unlawful Employment Practices

The heart of Title VII is stated in the first four subsections of 2000e-2 indicating what employment practices are illegal for each of the stated entities.

It is unlawful for an employer to fail or refuse to hire or to discharge any individual, or otherwise to discriminate against any individual with regard to conditions of employment, because of such individual's race, color, religion, sex, or national origin. It is also unlawful to limit, segregate, or classify employees or applicants for employment in any way that would deprive or tend to deprive any individual of employment opportunities or otherwise adversely affect his or her status as an employee, because of that individual's race, color, religion, sex, or national origin.

It should be quite clear that the Act protects only the five stated categories and only in the context of employment. It is not a panacea for all types of discrimination. It does not protect against discrimination in business dealings, and does not protect individuals who are not employees, such as independent contractors. Other acts may provide protection against other types of discrimination, but Title VII must be understood to provide protection in the limited area of employment for the five stated categories. The five categories require some elucidation.

a. Race. This term embodies the traditional ethnological races such as Negroid, Caucasian, Oriental, and so forth, but also includes categories not scientifically recognized as races. It would include Hispanics or semitic peoples even though they are not identified necessarily with a distinct "race."

b. Color. Color certainly overlaps with race but provides protection where race would not. For example, Cape Verdeans are of Portuguese ancestry but their complexions are dark. Thus, they would not normally qualify for protection by reason of race, but would for color. Color would also extend to cases where a lighter skin was preferred in people of the same race.

c. Religion. Over the years the courts have coped with the concept of what constitutes religion with increasingly liberal interpretations. For the purposes of Title VII, the EEOC has taken a very liberal concept of who is included in the term. It obviously includes the recognized faiths such as Judaism, Roman Catholicism, Protestantism, Islam, Buddhism, and so forth, but also included are moral and ethical beliefs as to what is right and wrong that are sincerely held with the strength of traditional religious views. The fact that no religious group espouses such beliefs or the fact that the religious group to which the individual professes to belong may not accept that belief is not determinative of the issue. The definition includes atheists, agnostics, and Deists, but does not include persons whose beliefs stem from a political or sociological position. Discussion of that distinction is beyond the scope of the present work, but it is a fascinating area for philosophical discourse.

The term "religion" includes all aspects of religious observance as well as belief. These observances need not be mandated by a particular religion and will be protected if undertaken in good faith in behalf of a religion. Examples would include the wearing of a cross or a yarmulke. The Act specifically requires an employer to make reasonable accommodation for religious observances unless unable to do so without undue hardship.

A reasonable accommodation is any accommodation that resolves the conflict, it is hoped, although not necessarily, to the satisfaction of the employee. If there are alternative accommodations, the EEOC guidelines provide that the employer must choose the one least disadvantageous to the employment opportunities of the employee. However, the Supreme Court has indicated that the only obligation an employer has is to provide a reasonable accommodation to the employee, and any reasonable accommodation will meet the obligations of the Act.[12] Efforts on the part of an employer to arrange for voluntary substitutes and swaps, to provide flexible scheduling, and to arrange lateral transfers and changes of job assignments would constitute reasonable accommodations. As noted, an employer is required to make a reasonable accommodation unless the accommodation results in undue hardship.

Undue hardship is not defined in the Act, but in the key case *Trans World Airlines, Inc. v. Hardison*,[13] the Supreme Court indicated that minimal hardship will constitute "undue" hardship. Since that case the EEOC has adopted guidelines that embody the findings in *Hardison*.[14] The guidelines deal with costs and seniority rights. Costs that are more than *de minimis* costs are undue. The guidelines suggest that the continued payment of premium wages to a substitute worker would be more than *de minimis*. However, infrequent payments of premium wages would not be an undue hardship. The guidelines also take the position that administrative costs involving the rearrangement of schedules would not constitute more than a *de minimis* cost.

The *Hardison* case also involved the question of whether the Act required the disruption of a contracted for, bona fide seniority system in order to provide accommodation. Since the request for voluntary substitutes was unavailing in Hardison's case, a requirement of assigning someone more senior would have the effect of discriminating against that individual in order to make the accommodation. The Supreme Court found that unacceptable and the EEOC has adopted that position in its guidelines.

Title VII exempts religious organizations from the requirement not to discriminate in the employment of individuals on the basis of religion. The wording of the particular section[15] suggests that all entities of the religion, whether involving religious activity or not, are covered by the exemption. The Supreme Court has upheld this view in *Corporation of the Presiding Bishop v. Amos*.[16] However, religious organizations are not exempt from other requirements of Title VII if they meet the definition for "employer."

d. Sex. Under Title VII sex is understood to mean gender and not practices or proclivities. Thus, for example, homosexuals are not protected. Nor would it be discriminatory under the Act to fire a woman who lived as wife and husband with a man not legally her husband, providing the policy applied to both sexes. The 1978 amendments to Title VII added the interpretation of the terms "because of sex" and "on the basis of sex" to include pregnancy, childbirth, or related medical conditions.

The EEOC guidelines[17] recognize sex as a bona fide occupational qualification but require this exception to be interpreted narrowly. It is permissible, for instance, to hire individuals of a particular sex, such as actors, for the purpose of authenticity and genuineness. Presumably it would be permissible to assign only female rest room attendants to women's rest rooms if there was a similar policy of assigning only male attendants to men's rest rooms, although even this would invite scrutiny into the actual nature of the jobs. Few libraries utilize rest room attendants, and no other library positions come to mind that would qualify for the BFOQ exemption. Certainly it would be improper to refuse to hire a woman on the basis of an assumption such as that the turnover rate is higher for women than men. Hiring on the basis of stereotypes is also impermissible. For instance, hiring on the theory that women can do intricate work better or that women can file better is impermissible. The question is whether the particular individual who is applying for a job can do that job. There are many stereotypes concerning the appropriateness of certain jobs for certain sexes but these must give way to the ability of an individual to perform the task in question. In the library setting, these stereotypes may take the form of beliefs that women can type better, that women are better at secretarial work, or that women are better as children's librarians. Librarians are not, unfortunately, immune to these stereotypical beliefs.

e. National Origin. The EEOC includes under this rubric the place where an individual or his or her ancestors originated. But the coverage is actually broader than that. The Commission will carefully scrutinize discrimination that is grounded in national origin considerations, such as the individual's marriage to, or association with, persons of a national origins group, or even if the person has a name suggestive of a national origins group but is not, in fact, of that national origin.

While the occasion is not too likely to arise in a library setting, American-born persons (Anglos) are also protected from discrimination on the basis of national origin. For example, a library in a Texas town bordering on Mexico that has a high proportion of Mexican-Americans cannot prefer to hire Mexican-Americans over Americans of a different ancestry. Puerto Rico presents an interesting situation, in that Puerto Ricans are American citizens and seemingly it would not be possible, on a national origin basis, to discriminate between natives of the island and continental Americans. The courts have recognized, however, the distinctive difference of the Puerto Rican heritage, and found that discrimination can be found in treatment between natives of the island and continental Americans.[18]

Speak-English-only rules are regarded as suspect by the EEOC.[19] When applied at all times, it is viewed as a violation of Title VII. One's native tongue is a characteristic of one's national origin, and to forbid the use of it disadvantages the individual's employment opportunities, because this may be the most effective way for the individual to communicate and may create an atmosphere of inferiority, isolation, and intimidation. An employer may impose an English-only rule at certain times as a business necessity such as when dealing with the public. Few libraries would be faced with the situation, although communities bordering Mexico might need to be alert to the problem. Presumably, libraries in Puerto Rico would have the same problem if they required speak-Spanish-only rules. No cases on this have come to light.

General Title VII Principles

Title VII guidelines refer in numerous places to Title VII principles. The term "Title VII principles" incorporates two distinct types of discrimination: disparate treatment and disparate (sometimes adverse) impact.

Disparate treatment arises when a qualified individual in one of the five protected classes is denied a benefit because of his or her race, color, religion, sex, or national origin. *McDonnell Douglas v. Green*[20] set the paradigm for the analysis of such cases. The plaintiff has the obligation of establishing a *prima facie* case by proving (1) that he or she is a member of one of the protected classes, (2) that he or she applied for a job (or promotion, etc.) for which the employer was seeking applicants, (3) that he or she was qualified for the position, (4) that he or she was denied the position, and (5) that the employer continued to seek applicants. Plaintiff having established this, the defendant must put forward a legitimate nondiscriminatory reason for rejection of the plaintiff.

There are any number of legitimate reasons that might be put forward, if in fact they are true and applied uniformly. Examples include a poor past record, long absence from the line of work, history of absenteeism, and failure to pass objective tests. These criteria must be applied uniformly and in a nondiscriminatory manner. Upon articulating the nondiscriminatory reason for not hiring the individual, the burden returns to the plaintiff to prove that the reason proffered is merely a pretext.

Proof that the application of an employment policy is pretextual can be found where the employer does not apply the "pretext" equally to all applicants and employees, or where the policy results in a workforce not reflective of the population from which that workforce is drawn. Disparate treatment is the result of an intent to discriminate, or at the very least, an ignorance of obligations in the hiring and treatment of employees. For example, the nineteenth-century notice that "Irish need not apply" would clearly be unlawful under Title VII. But an employer would not be justified in turning away an Irish person on the grounds that the necessary quota of Irish had already been hired. The fact is that each individual has a right to fairness in employment and the benefits of employment regardless of the status of the existing labor force. While undoubtedly bigotry exists in libraries, disparate treatment is probably not a major form of discrimination there, although any instance is intolerable.

Disparate impact, however, is an area that needs more careful monitoring, for a discriminatory result can arise out of policies instituted with the best of motives. Disparate impact occurs when a policy, neutral on its face, has the effect of limiting opportunities for persons within one of the protected groups. For example, a height requirement that all applicants for a position be at least five feet eight inches tall is neutral in that all applicants must meet the requirement, but obviously the impact of the rule is to discriminate against women as they are typically shorter than men. Such a rule would probably discriminate against people of certain national origins also.

The leading case on disparate impact is *Griggs v. Duke Power Co.*[21] The Duke Power Company, a North Carolina corporation, evidently decided to upgrade its workforce by requiring applicants to have a high school diploma and to pass two professionally recognized tests, one of which purported to test intelligence and the other mechanical comprehension. These tests were required of all applicants and thus were neutral as to their application. However, the impact of the rule disadvantaged blacks for as a group, blacks held proportionally fewer high school diplomas than did whites in North Carolina, and blacks routinely do less well on standardized tests, presumably because of cultural bias in the test. *Griggs* found this to be unlawful and established (1) that neutral employment qualifications will be judged by their impact and not by the good faith in which they were instituted, (2) that once discriminatory impact is established, the employer carries the burden of proving that the qualifications are justified by objective proof that they constitute a "business necessity," and (3) that "business necessity" is to be judged in terms of the particular individual's ability to perform the job which the employer is seeking to fill.

As noted, an employer who has instituted a neutral policy that has an adverse impact on persons within one of the protected groups may defend the policy on the ground that it is a business necessity. In libraries generally there are not too many jobs whose nature requires a policy that results in discrimination. One can imagine a facility in which the stacks are so high that all applicants for shelvers' jobs are required to be at least six feet tall, which would surely adversely impact women and certain racial groups, but which would pass muster as a business necessity.

In all cases, the key to viability of the business necessity defense is that the discriminatory requirement have a manifest relationship to the job to be performed. Such things as height requirements, lifting ability, stamina, previous experience, educational qualifications, and criminal records may tend to disadvantage one or more of the groups protected under Title VII. If a business necessity for the policy cannot be found, the Act will have been violated. The Act requires a careful look at policies that may look like prudent personnel practices.

Many establishments, and libraries could easily be among them, have policies against hiring persons with records of arrest, indictment, or conviction of crimes. Such a policy has the effect of being discriminatory toward those groups that have a disproportionally high rate of incidences of criminal conduct. To have such a policy is to violate Title VII, unless it is applied within the strictures of the business necessity exception. Some crimes, of course, may be so violent as to raise legitimate questions of safety for fellow employees and patrons without regard to particular job requirements. However, one generally needs to look at the nature of the crime in relation to the requirements of the job. Conviction for drunk driving might well disqualify any applicant for a position of driving the bookmobile, but it should not disqualify a person for work in special collections. On the other hand, conviction for theft might bar one from working with rare books but not from working in circulation.

Educational qualifications inevitably disadvantage minority groups, and the imposition of such qualifications must also meet the "business necessity" exception to avoid violating Title VII. As a general rule, the courts will look closely at educational requirements for unskilled and semiskilled jobs, but as jobs entail more responsibility and become more supervisory and managerial, the courts will allow an assumption that a certain level of education can be required for certain positions. The requirement of the professional degree for a professional position is rarely questioned, for the degree represents the acquisition of skills and knowledge necessary for performance in the job. The courts have upheld the requirement for the appropriate degree for social workers, laboratory technicians, public health employees, forestry agents, and professional librarians.[22]

Libraries, of course, employ individuals running the gamut of skills. It is obvious from the foregoing discussion that libraries can demand the professional library degree of applicants for professional positions, and presumably, though not a Title VII question, can require that that degree be from an accredited library school. Requirements for additional subject degrees would also be permissible for subject specialists. However, below the professional ranks, educational requirements become increasingly questionable as the positions decrease in skill and responsibility. While there is no case in point, it probably would pass muster to require a college degree of, say, a circulation desk manager, if the job entailed responsibilities of personnel assignments, work flow coordination, and training in computerized circulation control. Although no liberal arts program trains an individual for such work, this appears to be "white collar" work for which the courts tend to think a college degree is "necessary."[23]

Educational requirements for clerical positions are highly questionable. The courts have come down on both sides of the question, but the EEOC is quite consistent in its position that educational requirements for ordinary clerical positions are discriminatory toward minority groups. There is undoubtedly the reaction that anyone who fails to graduate from high school will also fail in other undertakings, but that is an assumption that library administrators may not make. The question is not the negative factor of failure to achieve a goal, but the positive one of whether an individual can do a particular job. The easy assumption that a certain level of education assures competence does not suffice. Indeed, in an era in which a high school diploma does not assure that the individual can read, it seems only right that an individual's capabilities and not his or her credentials be considered. If, of course, the clerical job should entail responsibilities such as supervision of personnel or finances, this might allow for a requirement of attainment of a certain educational level.

Bona Fide Occupational Qualifications

Bona fide occupational qualifications (BFOQ) can be an important exception to the rules against discrimination in certain enterprises, but as noted in the discussion of sex above, libraries are not among them. It is difficult, though perhaps not impossible, to imagine a library position that requires a particular race, sex, color, or national origin. For those interested in fine legal distinctions, there is a difference between BFOQ and business necessity. The BFOQ exception is discriminatory from the outset. A particular position, for example a role in a play, may require a white male actor and, if so, it is permissible to discriminate against women and people of color to fill that position. The courts are very careful to demand that the discriminatory requirement goes to the essence of the enterprise, but if it does, it is permissible. The business necessity exemption arises from practices that are neutral on their face but discriminatory in practice, such as a height requirement that would tend to disadvantage women and those of particular national origins and possibly races. The courts tend to require a higher standard for the BFOQ that must fulfill an *essential* function, whereas to satisfy a business necessity, there need be only a "manifest relationship" between the regulation and job performance.

Remedies and Enforcement Procedures

Title VII provides the courts with broad discretion to "make whole" a victim of discrimination.[24] The courts may, but are not limited to, the award of back pay, hiring or reinstatement, seniority, punitive and compensatory damages, attorneys' and experts' fees,[25] "or any other equitable relief as the court deems appropriate."

The procedures for enforcing one's rights under Title VII are moderately complicated and intricate. Those details need not be covered here, for the simple fact is that any employee who believes he or she is the victim of discrimination should seek out a lawyer immediately. However, every employee needs to know something about the timeframe within which a complaint must be made, for failure to file a complaint within the statute of limitations is, in nearly all cases, fatal. The key fact to remember is that the statute of limitations is very short.

In states where there is no state or local agency for the enforcement of fair employment practices, a claim of discrimination under Title VII must be filed with the EEOC within 180 days of the discriminatory act. Upon receipt of the claim the EEOC will notify the employer of the complaint, and will initiate an investigation within ten days of receipt of the claim. If the investigation fails to find reasonable cause to believe that the charge is true, the Commission will dismiss the charge and notify the parties. The charging party is also notified that it has a right to bring a private suit within ninety days of the notice to vindicate its charge. If, on the other hand, it appears that there is reasonable cause to believe the charge is true, the Commission will attempt to eliminate the problem through informal methods such as conference, conciliation, and persuasion.

The Commission has exclusive jurisdiction over the matter for 180 days after the charge is filed with the EEOC. The first thirty days are devoted to the attempt at informal reconciliation, after which the Commission (or where the respondent is the government, governmental agency or political subdivision, the Attorney General) may, if no acceptable agreement has been reached, file a civil action in the appropriate United States district court. If the government chooses not to file suit or has not at the end of 180 days, the Commission or the Attorney General, as the case may be, should notify the complainant and issue a right-to-sue letter if requested. The complainant then has a ninety-day period in which to file suit. The expiration of the 180-day period merely ends the government's exclusive jurisdiction, and if the complainant does not receive a letter to sue, the government retains the right to sue and the complainant retains the right to sue almost without time limitation.

In states where there is a state or local agency for the enforcement of fair employment practices (so-called deferral agencies), the claim should be filed with that agency. The state agency then has sixty days of exclusive jurisdiction over the charge in which to resolve the problem, although it can terminate its jurisdiction sooner. At the end of the state agency's jurisdiction, if no resolution has been reached, the individual may, within thirty days of notice that state jurisdiction has been terminated, file his or her complaint with the EEOC. Because of the state agency involvement, the time in which the claim must be filed with the EEOC is increased to 300 days from the date of the discriminatory act. Simple arithmetic indicates that the claim should be filed with the state agency before the expiration of 240 days, so that if the state agency uses its full sixty days of exclusive jurisdiction, there still will be time to file with the EEOC. Once the claim is filed with the EEOC, the procedures outlined above are followed.

As a general rule, the time in which to file a claim with the EEOC starts counting from the date of the act of discrimination. There are, however, situations in which the individual is unaware that the act was discriminatory until a later date, in which case courts will find a date when the person knew or should have known of the discriminatory act.[26] In a situation in which an employee had several months notice of termination if certain (discriminatory) conditions were not met, the court determined that the period to file began to run on the date of the actual termination and not on the date of notice to do so.[27] There are also continuing violations such as pay discrimination that recur every payday. Continuing violations will allow the employee to begin to count the period in which to file the claim from the last date of the discriminatory act.[28] While the continuing violation extends the filing period forward, it does not allow a complainant to collect for a longer period back on the grounds that the discrimination began earlier.[29] As noted above, the matter is complicated and requires the assistance of a competent lawyer. Employers need only note the various deadlines as a defense.

Sexual Harassment
Background

Sexual harassment is a relatively recently recognized form of discrimination. The term itself seems to have entered the vocabulary in the mid-1970s, at about the same time that courts began to recognize that this was a form of discrimination covered by Title VII's prohibition of discrimination in employment on the basis of sex.[30] It was 1980 when the EEOC issued its first set of guidelines on sexual harassment,[31] and it was as recently as 1986 that the U.S. Supreme Court first decided a case on the issue of sexual harassment.[32] Seemingly, it was not until the testimony of Professor Anita Hill in the fall of 1991, during the hearings on the nomination of Clarence Thomas to the Supreme Court, that the entire nation became aware of the enormity and pervasiveness of the matter.

Sexual harassment is, of course, not a recent phenomenon; only the recognition that it is a matter for legal protection is recent. Title VII of the Civil Rights Act of 1964 is the major piece of legislation dealing, on the federal level, with sexual harassment, and it only deals with one particular area of sexual harassment, that which takes place in connection with employment. There are other areas in which the vulnerable are preyed upon sexually by the more powerful. Included here are such relationships as attorney/client, doctor/patient, teacher/student, and parson/parishioner, among others. There are varying mechanisms that attempt to deal with the problem: professional associations can levy sanctions, many state governors have issued executive orders that reach state employees, some states have legislation, and there is public pressure, although a matter has to become public for this last to be effective.

Sexual Harassment in Employment

Sexual harassment is *unwelcome* sexual conduct that is a condition of employment. The EEOC is careful to note that Title VII does not proscribe all conduct of a sexual nature that is related to the workplace. Indeed, it can safely be assumed that many lasting relationships with a sexual component have blossomed between people brought together in a work environment and therefore it is vital to distinguish between welcome and unwelcome sexual conduct. Sexual harassment is understood to include two fairly separate types: "quid pro quo" and "hostile environment."

Quid Pro Quo

Quid pro quo harassment occurs when an employment decision is based on the provision or rejection of sexual favors demanded of the employee by an individual with the authority, real or apparent, to affect the employment decision, and such favors are unwelcome. Three things come together under quid pro quo harassment: the advance must be of a sexual nature, the advance must be unwelcome, and there must be an adverse employment decision, either actual or implied, arising from the advance. Note that the first two elements alone may be enough to constitute a hostile environment.

The Advance Must Be Sexual

Title VII and other antidiscrimination acts bar harassment based on race, color, religion, gender, national origin, age, and disability. The EEOC has promulgated proposed guidelines concerning such harassment but has, at the same time, recognized a distinction among types of harassment, finding sexual harassment a matter apart because it raises issues about human interaction that are not seen in other types of harassment. These proposed rules do not supersede the guidelines on sexual harassment issued in 1980, which remain in effect, but they do put in guideline form the EEOC's position that sex harassment is not limited to harassment that is sexual in nature, but also includes harassment due to gender-based animosity. By its very nature, however, quid pro quo harassmant is purely sexual.[33]

In the context of quid pro quo sexual harassment, the usual situation is a proposition for an overt sex act coupled with an overt or tacit threat of job reprisal. However, a finding of quid pro quo harassment does not require a blatant sex act or request for one. One court found quid pro quo harassment where a supervisor grabbed an employee, kissed her, and said she would go far if she did the right things.[34] On the other hand, courts will not find sexual harassment in simple, albeit repeated, invitations to dine or to see clients at the employer's home.[35] The question is judged by an objective standard that asks whether the reasonable person would have found the conduct to be sexual in nature.[36]

The Advance Must Be Unwelcome

In order for harassment to be found, the advance must be unwelcome. Obviously if one welcomes a sexual advance there can be no harassment, at least to the parties in the particular encounter. Unwelcome, however, does not mean that compliance with the advance is not voluntary, at least as the courts view the situation. The act is voluntary in that one has a valid choice: one can submit to the demand for sex or one can be fired (or whatever detriment is threatened). With this line of thinking a woman who submits to a rapist rather than be killed does so voluntarily. Clearly the reasoning is flawed, but the result, in the case of harassment, benefits the person harassed. The first defense anyone would raise in a sexual harassment situation, as with a rape case, is that the woman was willing. With rape that is sufficient, if proved, to exonerate the defendant, but in sexual harassment it is not, because the courts will say, yes, she was willing, but did she regard it as undesirable or offensive? As the Supreme Court said in *Meritor Savings Bank v. Vinson*,[37] the "gravamen of any sexual harassment claim is that the alleged sexual advances were 'unwelcome.'"

Determining Whether Sexual Conduct Is Unwelcome

The EEOC has noted that there are gradations in acceptance of sexual advances, ranging from those that are invited, to the uninvited but welcome, to offensive but tolerated, to the flatly rejected. The distinctions can be difficult to discern, but as noted previously, they are crucial. As with any evidence, corroborating witnesses are very helpful to a complainant; an analysis of the totality of the circumstances may shed light on the situation, but the matter may turn solely on the credibility of the two parties directly involved.

A contemporaneous complaint will bolster the complainant's case, although a lack of complaint or protest prior to the formal charge calls for an investigation into the reasons why no protest was made when harassment began.

In assessing welcomeness, any past conduct on the part of the complainant must relate directly to the alleged harasser. Past sexual intercourse with another supervisor would not be probative in a situation with another supervisor, nor would the fact that a complainant was known to have used foul language herself in a consensual setting be a reason to waive her protection against unwanted sexual harassment.[38] However, at least one court has allowed evidence of an *employer's* past record of sexual harassment to be admitted into evidence as it was deemed relevant to his intent in dismissing the complainant.[39]

A particularly difficult situation arises when sexual conduct starts out as welcome and becomes unwelcome as the ardor between the parties cools. The complainant has the burden of proving that any further sexual conduct is unwelcome, work-related harassment. Another complication arises from a situation in which, at the termination of a consensual affair, the employee is fired. Some courts will find that, unless the employer made threats to fire the employee unless the sexual favors continued, the firing was not sexual harassment because sexual favors are no longer being sought. Such a firing is seen as a rather harsh reaction to the ending of the affair but not sexual harassment.[40] Other courts view the firing as flowing from the sexual affair, and will find the firing sexual harassment.[41]

Hostile Environment as Sexual Harassment

The Supreme Court in *Meritor Savings Bank v. Vinson* recognized that Title VII protected against a sexually oppressive work environment as well as the "quid pro quo" sexual harassment discussed above. The Court in that case noted that the sexual harassment, to be actionable, "must be sufficiently severe or pervasive as to alter the conditions of the victim's employment and create an abusive working environment" (at 67). Clearly, this suggests that isolated remarks, the occasional use of vulgar language, or a single touch on the arm is usually insufficient to constitute sexual harassment.

The EEOC and some courts have suggested that a number of elements be analyzed to determine whether conditions are severe or pervasive enough to qualify as sexual harassment. There is the question whether the unwanted sexual attention is verbal or physical, with the idea that unwanted touching is usually more offensive than words. There is the frequency of offensive encounters to be considered. One might look to the length of time over which the offensive acts occurred and the context in which they occurred. None of this advice is very helpful, as in itself it offers no guidelines and leaves one to wonder what degree of verbal abuse equals a pat on the rear end or how often something needs to happen to become frequent. The answer lies in reliance on the "reasonable person." It may salve one's conscience to believe that one has reached the conclusion of the reasonable person through an analysis of salient factors, but in reality, the conclusion reached is one's own gut reaction to the totality of the situation. As noted above, this raises the interesting question of whether the standard ought to be the "reasonable woman" rather than the "reasonable person," and certainly not, one presumes, the "reasonable man." A strong theoretical argument can be made for this, but in practical terms recent cases that have reached the courts are so outrageous that the outcome would not change regardless of which reasonable entity was the standard.

Types of Activity Contributing to a Hostile Environment

The EEOC Guidelines issued in 1980 state specifically that sexual harassment includes conduct that "has the purpose or effect of unreasonably interfering with an individual's work performance or creating an intimidating, hostile, or offensive working environment."[42] The guidelines do not suggest exactly what activity is proscribed, undoubtedly because there is no end to the possibilities. Actual cases brought forward suggest that the harassment can be roughly classified as physical or violent acts; vulgar or indecent language; sexual remarks, requests, and pictures; and required use of provocative clothing.

Physical or Violent Acts. Physical or violent acts may, of course, be a part of "quid pro quo" discrimination, but if perpetrated by persons not in a position of authority and thus not resulting in any imposed employment detriment, protection must come because of a poisoned employment environment. To be actionable the conduct must be sufficiently severe or pervasive as to alter the conditions of the victim's employment and to create an abusive working environment. In the *Meritor* case a supervisor made repeated demands on his female subordinate for sexual favors. It was charged that she had sexual intercourse with him forty or fifty times, that he fondled her in front of other employees, followed her into the women's rest room when she went there alone, exposed himself to her, and forcibly raped her on several occasions, all of which the court determined to be sufficient to create a hostile working environment. This would seem to be an extreme situation; the question is how much less pervasive can the acts be to sustain a finding of hostile environment.

One court found that a claim of sexual harassment by an employee whose immediate supervisor's actions included patting her bottom, touching her in the breast area, and attempting to have an affair with her while they attended a job-related convention was insufficient to establish a prima facie case of sexual harassment.[43] However, courts will consider nonsexual aggression as part of the prohibited pattern of sexual discrimination. In a particularly disgusting case female flaggers who were assigned to a construction site were subjected to sexually suggestive epithets, constantly asked to engage in sexual intercourse, touched against their will, and "mooned"; the men also exposed themselves, and urinated in the gas tank of one woman's car.[44] The upshot of all this seems to be that sexual byplay of a reasonably innocuous character will be tolerated, whereas excessive importunings, especially when coupled with outrageous hazing, will be found to satisfy the requirements of sexual harassment. As an aside, it is interesting to note that the *Hall* case is devoid of sex in the erotic sense. There is the touching and the requests for sex, but it is all considered in the character of demeaning the women rather than proposing or promoting actual sexual encounters. One can ponder the question of whether the courts might not consider this merely the give and take of a rough industry had there not been the existence of a seemingly sexual character to the matter. But is the matter sexually- or even gender-based? Suppose the flaggers had been male and undergone the same sort of harassment. How then ought the courts to treat the matter?

Vulgar or Indecent Language. Harassment in the form of verbal comment is recognized by the courts as a type of sexual discrimination. Numerous harangues of demeaning sexual inquiries coupled with repeated requests for sexual relations have been found sufficient to sustain a prima facie case,[45] and an employer is liable for vulgar and indecent language directed toward women even though that language is tolerated and even participated in by some women.[46] The complainant herself, as seems obvious, cannot be a willing participant in whatever verbal byplay might be found offensive by others,[47] but one must always be careful to determine whether participation, although "voluntary" in the sense that it is not coerced, is unwelcome.[48] There is, of course, the question of how sustained and pervasive the language must be to support a finding that the language is sufficient to create an oppressive work environment. A single incident in which a plant manager commented about a female employee's breasts failed to convince one court that the incident, although unseemly, was outrageous enough to create a hostile environment.[49]

Required Use of Provocative Clothing. In the period when minidresses were fashionable and thought shocking by a few, an occasional librarian ran afoul of some trustee's dress code, but there is no evidence that any library administration ever required the wearing of provocative clothing or revealing costumes, and it seems unlikely to happen in the foreseeable future. That being the case, little need be said of the matter here. Still, it may be a form of sexual harassment and so a brief mention is in order.

The EEOC takes the position that required costumes become sexual harassment when (1) the outfit is sexually provocative or revealing and (2) wearing the outfit is likely to result in the wearer's being subjected to unwelcome verbal or physical sexual activity.[50]   For example, one court found sexual harassment where an employer required a female lobby attendant to wear an outfit with slits in the dress that revealed portions of her thighs and buttocks; the outfit, commemorating the national Bicentennial and featuring a flag motif, prompted visitors to the lobby to whistle "Yankee Doodle" and "The Stars and Stripes Forever," and one person offered to "run it up the flagpole any time you want to."[51]   While this complainant was expected to wear the outfit over a period of days, cases are not consistent on whether the dress requirement needs to be more than a one-time occurrence.   One court found that a single occurrence of an employer's request for a waitress to remove the skirt she wore over her leotards was insufficient to support a claim of sexual harassment,[52] but the EEOC determined that a requirement, on a single occasion, that a female employee wear a "special" hostess costume consisting of halter-bra top and midiskirt with split in front running up to her thighs was sufficient to support a claim, perhaps because there was also evidence that the employee had been subjected to numerous sexual advances by her supervisor.[53]   In reality the deciding factor is the totality of the situation, which involves an analysis of the constituent elements to determine whether the harassment is "sufficiently severe or pervasive" as to create "an abusive work environment."

Pictures, Cartoons, and Graffiti of a Sexual Nature. The presence of pictorial matter depicting sexual activity, suggesting lust, focusing on genitalia, or merely showing nudity can be the basis for a hostile environment.   It is undoubtedly true that the workplaces of traditionally male-predominant occupations were often awash with such examples of the graphic arts, but it does little to assuage the sensibilities of women lately come to that workforce to know that men have always seen women in a demeaning light.   Such depictions must seem directed personally at female employees, and clearly the situation is vastly exacerbated when the artwork is particularized toward an individual female, usually by adding her name.

As with other factors constituting harassment, there is always the question of how much of the particular thing is required to constitute the pervasiveness sufficient to create a hostile environment. Presumably the "reasonable woman" needs again to be considered, but in any event, the environment must be such that it would adversely affect the reasonable person. One court found an indecent picture with the plaintiff's name on it in the men's room sufficient to be harassment.[54] Most cases involve other forms of harassment along with the pictorial content. In a particularly egregious case a female police officer had to face not only pictures of sexual intercourse with her name written on the pictures, but constant threats about her job and other nonsexual harassment such as other officers parking their cars so close to the driver's side of her car that she couldn't enter the vehicle from that side and male dispatchers calling her in to the station for no reason. Such acts of harassment were not only condoned by her superiors but were perpetrated by them, including the chief of police. The result was that, finally, the woman could not continue to work and required psychiatric care.[55]

In terms of its effect on an individual, *Arnold* is difficult to top, for the harassment was focused on a particular individual, it was concentrated, and it was persistent, with the dire result noted above. For overall pervasiveness, however, it would be difficult to outdo *Robinson v. Jacksonville Shipyards, Inc.*[56]

Testimony in the trial indicated that there were dozens, if not hundreds (the testimony often indicates "pictures" without giving a number), of pictures of nude or partially nude women in sexually provocative poses from calendars, centerfolds, and the like hung on walls throughout the shipyard facility. Additionally, pictorial periodicals such as *Playboy*, *Hustler*, and *Penthouse* were much in evidence, and the pictures in them were often shown to plaintiff Lois Robinson, to her disgust and evidently the glee of her male co-workers. Along with the pictorial display were sexual jokes, comments, and graffiti directed at Robinson, and on the part of some of her male co-workers, open hostility toward working with her.

The case is particularly interesting not only for its evidence of boorishness in the workplace, but for the evidence given by plaintiff's expert witnesses, D. Susan Fiske and Ms. K. C. Wagner, which provides a theoretical framework by which the harm engendered by a sexually abusive atmosphere and reactions to the harm can be understood. The case also includes a sexual harassment policy written for the Jacksonville Shipyards, Inc. that would be an excellent model for anyone engaged in creating such a policy. In short, the case is an excellent study of the hostile work environment situation, a reading of which would be highly educational.

Employer Liability

Title VII makes it an unlawful employment practice for an *employer* to discriminate against a protected person in that person's employment. Thus, it is necessary to implicate the employer in any hostile environment controversy to trigger Title VII, as Title VII does not protect an employee from the aggression of co-workers not acting as agents of the employer. There may and probably would be causes of action against harassing co-workers by such actions as assault, battery, and intentional infliction of emotional distress, but co-workers seldom have sufficient resources to make a suit worthwhile. Title VII itself applies to any "employer" or "any agent" of the employer.[57] The EEOC explicated this to mean that an employer was responsible for the acts of its agents and supervisors with respect to sexual harassment, "regardless of whether the specific acts complained of were authorized or even forbidden by the employer and regardless of whether the employer knew or should have known of their occurrence."[58] This amounts to strict liability, and the Supreme Court in

Meritor Savings Bank v. Vinson rejected this interpretation and stated that the general common law principles of *respondeat superior* should apply.

Respondeat superior translates into "let the master answer." The common law doctrine is that the master is responsible for the actions of his servants when they are acting within the scope of their duties. The usual defense, when subordinates do something wrong, is that they were not acting within the scope of their duties. The law goes beyond this, however, and will look to see whether the master knew or should have known of the activities of his under-lings. If it is found that the master either knew or should have known of the wrongful activities, and the master fails to take action to correct the situation, it is assumed that the action is in accord with the wishes of the master and the consequences thereof will be imputed to him. As one can imagine, however, the issue is seldom clearcut. Whether an employer knew or should have known of a condition is often in question, as is whether an employer's actions to avert or correct an undesirable condition are sufficient to shield him from liability.

The leading statement from the courts on employer liability is *Hicks v. Gates Rubber Co.*,[59] where the court relied on the *Restatement (Second) of Agency*. Under *Hicks* an employer is liable for the torts of the employee in any of three circumstances. First is when the employee is acting within the scope of his employment. The court noted that this provides scant assistance, for sexual harassment is never within one's job description.

A second, and far more useful rule, is found in employer negligence or recklessness in failure to remedy or prevent a hostile or offensive work envi-ronment. The first line of defense here would be to have a policy and set of procedures in place that are designed to prevent sexual harassment and to respond quickly and vigorously to a complaint when one does occur. The nature of the circumstances will determine acceptable alacrity. Immediate and same day action will always pass muster,[60] but waiting a day may incur a court's disapproval. Obviously, ineffective plans will be found unacceptable.[61]

Hicks identified a third area as a possible basis for employer liability for hostile work environment sexual harassment. Again relying on the *Restate-ment (Second) of Agency*, the court noted that the actions of the employee could be imputed to the employer where, although not within the scope of his duties, the employee had the apparent authority to act as he did. For example, a supervisor whose job description includes only oversight of work accom-plished and not job assignment may take it upon himself to assign work, and if he does it in a discriminatory manner that discrimination will be imputed to the employer unless the employer moves quickly to correct the situation.

Employer Responsibility

Every employer should develop and disseminate a policy for dealing with sex-ual harassment. Many libraries, as part of a larger organization, will have such policies already in place, but even then, there is an obligation to assure dissemination of that policy to all employees. The EEOC has stated that the best tool for the elimination of sexual harassment is prevention.[62] This involves affirmatively raising the subject, expressing strong disapproval, developing appropriate sanctions, informing employees of their right to raise and how to raise the issue of harassment under Title VII.

Any policy ought to include, at a minimum, a statement of the purpose of Title VII; a statement of prohibited conduct; a schedule of penalties for misconduct; and a set of procedures for making, investigating, and resolving sexual harassment and retaliation complaints. One would hope, of course, that procedures beyond educating employees to the problem would be unnecessary, and that awareness that there was a problem would effect an immediate resolution. Librarians are an intelligent and sensitive lot, but no administrator can assume that all library employees adhere to the golden rule in this area. Prudent policies should be in place.

Age Discrimination in Employment Act
Background

The Age Discrimination in Employment Act of 1967 (ADEA) was part of the civil rights legislation of the 1960s that included the Equal Pay Act, the Civil Rights Act of 1964, and the Voting Rights Act of 1965. Age had, in fact, been proposed as one of the protected categories in Title VII of the Civil Rights Act, but Congress ultimately rejected it, feeling that not enough was known to legislate intelligently in this area. In light of that, Congress directed the Secretary of Labor to undertake a study of the effects of discrimination in employment because of age and to report the findings therefrom. The study was done and the report issued in 1965. Subsequently, both houses of Congress conducted hearings of their own that agreed with the findings of the Secretary of Labor, and President Lyndon Johnson backed passage of the ADEA in his Older Americans Message delivered in 1967. The ADEA was enacted December 15, 1967, and became effective on June 12, 1968.

The Congressional findings stated in the Act were

1. that in the face of rising productivity and affluence, older workers find themselves disadvantaged in their efforts to retain employment, and especially to regain employment when displaced from jobs;
2. that the setting of arbitrary age limits regardless of potential for job performance has become a common practice, and certain otherwise desirable practices may work to the disadvantage of older persons;

3. that the incidence of unemployment, especially long-term unemployment with resultant deterioration of skill, morale, and employer acceptability, is, relative to the younger ages, high among older workers; their numbers are great and growing, and their employment problems grave;

4. that the existence, in industries affecting commerce, of arbitrary discrimination in employment because of age burdens commerce and the free flow of goods in commerce.

With these findings as background, findings that recognized not only the harm done to the individual older worker but also the resultant harm to the nation's commerce, the ADEA was passed with the purpose of promoting employment of older persons based on their ability rather than age, prohibiting arbitrary age discrimination in employment, and helping employers and workers find ways of meeting problems arising from the impact of age on employment.

Coverage

Employer

The ADEA applies to "employees" of "employers" as those terms are defined by the Act. An employer is any entity engaged in an industry affecting commerce who has twenty or more employees for each working day in twenty or more weeks during the current or preceding year. As with other civil rights acts, the term "industry affecting commerce" is very inclusive and reaches virtually every business enterprise. By definition, state and local governments are included in the term employer.

The Act also covers employment agencies and labor organizations, both as employers if they meet the criteria put forth in the Act, and in the activities they perform in employment placement.

Employees

Employees are persons employed by employers. This seemingly obvious fact is not quite as clear as it seems in some cases. The test of whether one is an employee, when a determination is necessary, involves the usual considerations: the basis of pay, the degree of control over the person's work, how social security taxes are paid, and so forth. Normally it is obvious that an individual is or is not an employee. Part-time employees are covered by the Act if their employer qualifies, but whether they are counted toward the twenty employees needed for an employer to come within the statute depends on the nature of the employment. Casual workers hired by the hour would not be included, but part-time workers who are continuously on the payroll would be. The key is whether an employment relationship exists between the individual and the employer and such a relationship does not require the individual worker to be full time.[63]

Religious Organizations and Private Clubs

Unlike some other civil rights acts that provide exemptions for religious organizations and private clubs, such as Title VII and the Americans with Disabilities Act, the ADEA makes no mention of religious organizations. Presumably both types of entities are covered by the ADEA if they qualify otherwise as employers. Private clubs clearly are not exempt from the ADEA, but religious institutions raise important First Amendment questions whenever the government seeks to regulate their internal affairs. The courts are quite consistent in not applying the Act to those closely involved in promulgating religious doctrine such as clergy and seminarians,[64] but there is less agreement where the entity is less directly involved in church doctrine.[65] It would be reasonable to assume that a library in a college offering general education that is affiliated with a religion would be covered by the ADEA. On the other hand, given the distinctions the Supreme Court has made over the years between religious education at the higher education level and elementary and secondary levels, the librarian in a parochial high school may not be protected by the ADEA.

What Discrimination Is Prohibited

The Act makes it discriminatory for a covered employer

1. to fail or refuse to hire or to discharge any individual or otherwise discriminate against any individual with respect to his compensation, terms, conditions, or privileges of employment, because of such individual's age;

2. to limit, segregate, or classify his employees in any way that would deprive or tend to deprive any individual of employment opportunities or otherwise adversely affect his status as an employee, because of such individual's age;

3. to reduce the wage rate of any employee in order to comply with this Act.

The ADEA coverage is broad in that it protects all "individuals" who are employees (with a few exceptions) and not just citizens. However, the protection extends only to employment situations and not to others, such as admittance to medical school or dealings with independent contractors. In the employment situation the coverage is inclusive and the Act proscribes all forms of discrimination based on age including wage benefits, hours worked, availability of overtime, and such benefits as educational opportunities, training programs, sick leave, vacations, and career development schemes.

The Protected Class

The ADEA protects employees who are at least 40 years of age. Earlier versions of the Act protected, at one time, persons 40 to 65 years of age. Sixty-five was later extended to 70 years of age and then, with the amendments of 1986, the upper age limit was eliminated. There are a few specific exceptions to this coverage.

The ADEA allows dismissal of high-ranking executives who have reached the age of 65, providing they have been in the position for the immediate two years prior to retirement and are immediately entitled to a retirement benefit of at least $44,000. The EEOC has made it clear that such executives must be truly high ranking, which envisions individuals who are responsible for the management of large numbers of employees and a large volume of business. Also, the retirement benefit of $44,000 is exclusive of Social Security benefits, employees' own contributions, rollover contributions, and contributions of prior employers. How many librarians meet both the definition of executive and the retirement figure is not known; probably some but not many.

The other specific exemptions to coverage apply to law enforcement officers and firefighters. Neither of these exemptions has application to libraries or librarians.

Prohibitions in Advertisements

The Act prohibits the publication of notices or advertisements for employment that indicate a preference, limitation, specification, or discrimination, based on age. Certain words suggesting youthfulness are generally suspect but their actual use will determine whether there is a violation of the statute. "Recent grads" in reference to a specific job opening would probably be a violation, whereas an ad appearing in June inviting "recent grads" to join the workforce through a particular agency would probably not be a violation. Other words and phrases that trigger alarms are "girls," "boys," "college students," and "young man," among many others. Phrases used for particular job openings such as "looking for a bright young girl" and "corporate attorney 1–2 years out of college" have been found by courts to be violative of the Act, but statements such as "junior" executive and "junior" secretary and "excellent first job" have been found to be descriptive of the positions involved and not suggesting younger applicants are desired.

Enforcement

Enforcement of the ADEA may be either by private civil action brought by any person aggrieved under the Act or by an action brought by the EEOC in behalf of the aggrieved person. Unlike Title VII, the person does not need a right-to-sue letter from the EEOC or any other sort of permission. However, if the EEOC does commence an action, the right of the individual to sue on his or her own behalf ceases. If a private suit has been filed prior to the commencement of a suit by the EEOC it will remain viable and not be dismissed unless the EEOC filing is very close in time. The courts aren't in agreement on the exact amount of time necessary to keep the private action alive. One private suit filed fourteen minutes prior to the EEOC's filing was dismissed,[66] as was a suit filed two days prior to the EEOC action.[67] However, an interval of twenty-six days was found to be sufficient to save a private suit from dismissal.[68]

Statute of Limitations

Prior to the Civil Rights Amendments of 1991, the ADEA provided a two-year statute of limitations for initiating lawsuits. The rule not only limited the period in which lawsuits could be filed, but limited the period for which economic recovery could be granted. This two-year statute was not harmonious with Title VII although, in most other respects, Title VII and the ADEA are very similar in scheme, especially in their charge-filing requirements. Because of the similarities between the statutes, the courts very often look to Title VII precedents in interpreting corresponding provisions of the ADEA; therefore, Congress determined it useful to conform the two statutes. To do that, Congress eliminated from the ADEA the two-year statute of limitations, which put the ADEA in line with Title VII whose only limitation is in the time allowed for filing charges.

The charge, a written statement identifying the parties and describing the discriminatory action, must be filed with the EEOC within 180 days of the alleged discriminatory act, or, in a state that has a law against discrimination in employment because of age and has an agency to handle such matters (a so-called deferral state), within 300 days of the alleged discriminatory act or within thirty days of notice to the individual of termination of proceedings under state law, whichever is earlier.

If the one who alleged discrimination because of age is in a deferral state, it is a requirement that the state be notified and given an opportunity, for a period of sixty days, to effect a remedy before suit can be filed in federal court. The individual then has the obligation of notifying the EEOC of the alleged discrimination and intent to sue. In a normal and orderly progression of things one would first inform the state and, if they failed to effect a resolution, go to the EEOC. If they, too, failed, the next step would be court. There is no requirement to go to the state first, however. One can first notify the EEOC and then the state, or one can file concurrently with the state and the EEOC. The only requirement is that one must file with both and wait out the sixty-day periods (unless terminated sooner) before filing with the court. One need not conform to any state requirement concerning the complaint other than a requirement of the filing of a written and signed statement of the facts upon which the proceeding is based. For example, one can miss a deadline for filing under state law and still preserve the right to sue in federal court, because the only requirement under the Act is to commence an action with the state and that is done when the filing is made, even if it is immediately thrown out as untimely.[70]

Upon notification, the EEOC has the obligation to notify all parties named in the charge as possible defendants in a suit, and must try to eliminate any alleged unlawful practice by informal methods of conciliation, conference, and persuasion. The aggrieved individual may not institute a civil action for sixty days while the EEOC is so engaged. If a charge filed with the EEOC is dismissed or otherwise terminated by the Commission, the Commission will so notify the aggrieved individual, who then has ninety days in which to file a civil suit. This ninety-day period will extend the statute of limitations if the notice is given within ninety days of the end of the limitations period or even after the statute has run its course. Any trial commenced is *de novo* and state agency or EEOC findings would have no bearing on it.

Establishing Violations

Anyone 40 years old or older who feels he or she has been discriminated against in some area of employment might easily assume that age had something to do with it, particularly if a younger person was the beneficiary of the act. The problem is proving the case, and what must be proved is that age was a determining factor in the decision, although there may have been other factors present.

Typically, the plaintiff will attempt, depending on the nature of the discriminatory act, to prove discriminatory intent by the wording in job notices and advertisements, and by finding notations on interview forms saying, "too old."[71] The mere fact that age was asked suggests a discriminatory intent.

Various tests required of all applicants might be discriminatory toward older applicants, and if not job related, could well be found discriminatory. Tests of strength are most obvious but mental tests too can be discriminatory, not because older persons have lost mental acuity but because they are further removed from schooling with its test-taking experiences and are less familiar with test taking. Educational requirements unrelated to the job might also be discriminatory toward older persons, who statistically have less education than younger persons.

In cases involving discharge or discipline of a person in the age-protected group for an infraction of a company rule, the action must be consistent with that meted out to other employees for similar infractions. The infraction may not be a pretext for an action actually based on the worker's age.

As with Title VII cases, the courts have structured two broad types of discrimination in the age area: disparate impact and disparate treatment. While the overwhelming number of cases in age discrimination are based on the disparate treatment theory[72] in which statistical evidence is less crucial, statistics may be used to prove that an employer has established a pattern or practice of discrimination. The courts have adopted for the ADEA statistical approaches developed under Title VII, but using statistics to prove age discrimination has turned out to be more difficult than proving other types of discrimination under Title VII. One reason is that the ADEA is not an affirmative action type of legislation. There is no requirement that an employer have or strive to have a work force representative by age level of society in general or of the particular labor pool from which the employer draws. Thus, statistics indicating that fewer older workers are employed tend not to be overly persuasive in refusal-to-hire cases. In dismissal cases the problem tends to be a lack of sufficient data to support a claim of discrimination. As one court pointed out, "for statistical evidence to be probative, however, the sample must be large enough to permit inference that age was a determinative factor in the employer's decision."[73] In this case, ten dismissals in eleven years was insufficient to be statistically significant. Certainly few libraries would have a turnover rate sufficient to establish statistically a pattern or practice of discrimination. Still, statistics may be useful, particularly in conjunction with other factors, in establishing a *prima facie* case of discrimination.

The Prima Facie *Case*

The usual, though certainly not the only, approach in age discrimination cases is the model established in *McDonnell Douglas Corp. v. Green,*[74] and refined in *Texas Dept. of Community Affairs v. Burdine,*[75] where the plaintiff must (1) present proof of being in the protected group; (2) present proof of being qualified for a position the employer sought to fill; (3) prove that an application for the job was made and rejected; (4) prove that the employer continued to seek applicants or that the job was filled by a younger person.

Once the plaintiff has presented this information, he or she is entitled to a favorable judgment unless the defendant can articulate a nondiscriminatory reason for the action taken. It would be a rare case in which the defendant could not come up with some reason, other than age, for the action taken. The reason must be clear and reasonably specific and have sufficient rational connection to the decision to allow a court to believe that it, rather than age, was the reason for the action taken. The Act provides two major defenses: reasonable factors other than age (sometimes referred to as RFOA) and bona fide occupational qualifications (always referred to as BFOQ). RFOAs present an almost endless list of reasons why an applicant wasn't hired or why an employee was disciplined or dismissed. Included in this list are failure to have the requisite qualifications, past criminal records, poor performance history in previous jobs, failure to pass qualifying tests, or, for persons already employed, poor job performance, infraction of company rules, tardiness, inflexibility in accepting new procedures, and reorganization or reduction in workforce. All of these would be reasonable factors for taking an action unfavorable to an applicant or employee provided that each action was decided upon in a fair and equitable manner. Reorganization may be a sound business judgment resulting in some layoffs of competent people, but if the decision as to who will be laid off is determined by advanced age, the process will not pass muster.

The other major defense provided by the Act is the BFOQ. Here the employer is saying, yes, age was the determining factor in my decision but it was necessary to the success of the business. The EEOC has indicated that BFOQs will have limited scope, and that as an exception to the Act, the concept must be narrowly construed.[76] In order to prevail, an employer asserting a BFOQ has the burden of proving that (1) the age limit is reasonably necessary to the essence of the business, and either (2) that all or substantially all individuals excluded from the job involved are in fact disqualified, or (3) that some of the individuals so excluded possess a disqualifying trait that cannot be ascertained except by reference to age.

Most of the cases asserting a BFOQ involve individuals whose positions involve public safety. Thus age is a BFOQ for commercial airline pilots, bus drivers, school bus drivers, law enforcement officers, and firefighters. Some courts have upheld maximum beginning hiring ages as BFOQs for law enforcement personnel and bus drivers, while other courts have rejected them.[77] To say the least, there is a decided lack of unanimity concerning age as a BFOQ, and the matter has not yet been given a unified reading by the Supreme Court. In any event, libraries are not likely to have any positions for which a BFOQ can be claimed.

At one time, "authenticity" was recognized by the regulations as promulgated by the Department of Labor as a BFOQ where theatrical productions and advertisements required individuals of a particular age for purposes of verisimilitude. When the EEOC replaced the Department of Labor as the enforcement agency, new guidelines were issued and excluded from them was any mention of "authenticity" as a BFOQ. Probably the omission is in recognition of the likelihood that such a situation would meet the general guidelines for BFOQs and needs no special illumination, but just maybe the EEOC thinks every casting call should be open to every age regardless of the character of the role to be filled. Auditions for diaper advertisements could be strange affairs indeed.

Once the defendant has presented his defense, which in most cases will be in the form of an RFOA, the burden shifts back to the plaintiff to prove that the reason proffered by the defendant was a pretext. This is by no means an impossible task. The reason proffered, of course, will determine what must be proved, but if that reason is untrue, presumably one can find evidence to unmask it. Also in the plaintiff's favor, the matter in most instances will be tried before a jury, and it is probably true that most juries are more sympathetic to the individual employee than to the more powerful employer.

Remedies

The Act states that "in any action brought to enforce this Act the court shall have jurisdiction to grant such legal or equitable relief as may be appropriate to effectuate the purposes of this Act, including without limitation judgments compelling employment, reinstatement or promotion, or enforcing the liability for amounts" due as back pay.[78] Other remedies include liquidated damages and front pay where appropriate. It is clear that the Act gives courts very broad powers of enforcement, but there are limits. Compensatory damages for such things as pain and suffering, emotional distress, humiliation, and injury to reputation are not available according to the majority of court decisions. A few courts have found otherwise.

Back Pay

The ADEA is remedial in outlook. It seeks to make the victim of discrimination "whole," that is, to put the victim in the economic position he or she would have been in had there been no discrimination. Back pay is the most obvious and probably the most used remedy. Whether the age-protected individual did not get the job or was fired from a job or was not promoted, there are economic consequences to the action and the victim has a right to what he or she should have got absent the discrimination. There is, of course, some obligation for the victim to mitigate damages by seeking and undertaking suitable employment while the suit is pending, and if the employee should win the suit, any award will be offset by the amount of money earned during the period. Suitable employment means a position requiring the education, skill, and experience the individual utilized in the job from which ousted or for which he or she was not selected. If the employer has been willful in discriminating, the victim can receive liquidated damages which is an additional amount equal to the amount arrived at for back pay.

What to include in back pay can raise problems. Wages would certainly be included, as well as fringe benefits and raises that all employees received. But what about commissions that may or may not have been earned or promotions that may or may not have been granted? What is the value of pension benefits the employee would have been earning had there been no discrimination and there was no reinstatement? (Reinstatement would put the person back in the retirement scheme where he or she had been, so the question of pension benefits would not arise.) The courts struggle with these questions and they do come up with answers. Usually. One appellate court, after struggling mightily with the problem of retirement benefits as back wages, remanded the case to the trial court saying, "This is a matter of some technicality, however, and one we leave largely to the trial court's discretion."[79]

Reinstatement

Reinstatement is an appropriate remedy for a wrongful discharge where the actual position formerly held by the victim is available or there is a comparable position to which the victim can be assigned. The courts are not in agreement as to the point at which "bumping" an innocent incumbent in order to reinstate a victim of age discrimination is an appropriate remedy. On the one hand, the replacement individual is (presumably) innocent of any wrongdoing and has legitimate expectations and a valid property interest in the job, but on the other hand, why should that individual have a greater claim to the job than the person who was wrongfully ousted as a result of discrimination?[80] Some courts have adopted the so-called "rightful place" theory, in which the victim of discrimination is given the right to the next available vacancy comparable to the job that was lost. This theory works well enough at mid-and lower-levels where vacancies open up with regularity, but at high levels where the position in question is the only one, bumping is the only alternative. Reinstatements involving seniority that could adversely impact on other employees without directly replacing them are not seen as a problem.[81]

Front Pay

Occasionally reinstatement is not an appropriate remedy, either because no opening exists or perhaps because the proceedings have so embittered the relationship between the employee to be reinstated and his or her supervisors or fellow workers that no fruitful working relationship is possible. In such situations courts will award front pay, for which the calculations are similar to those for back pay except that liquidated damages are not available. The length of time for which the award will be given is at the discretion of the court, but normally the award will be until some event reasonable for the particular circumstances occurs.[82] The award may be until an opening occurs for reinstatement, or until the employee reaches an age a few years hence at which he or she had expressed a desire to retire, or perhaps until a scheduled reorganization takes place in which the position is to be eliminated. In an appropriate situation the victim can receive both back pay and front pay.

Attorneys' Fees

Enforcement procedures of the ADEA incorporate features of the Fair Labor Standards Act, which provide that "The court shall, in addition to any judgment awarded to plaintiff, allow a reasonable attorney's fee to be paid by the defendant, and costs of the action" (29 U.S.C.A. s 216(b)). These are very important provisions, for on the one hand, competent attorneys are induced to undertake cases in which awards are generally quite small in the legal view of things, and costs would seriously eat into any award if not compensated for. While the language is somewhat discretionary, courts are actually very limited in their ability to deny attorneys' fees and costs to a winning plaintiff, but the determination of what is reasonable and what costs are actually covered gets very complicated and is beyond the scope of this work. As the ADEA provides for fees for prevailing plaintiffs only, a defendant cannot be awarded either attorneys' fees or costs.

Retaliation

The Act makes it unlawful for an employer to retaliate against an employee because that employee has opposed any practice made unlawful by the Act or has made a charge, testified, assisted, or participated in any manner in an investigation, proceeding, or litigation under the Act.[83]

Participation

Any employee taking part in an action under the ADEA is absolutely protected from retaliation for any participation in any proceeding relevant to the Act. An employer may not discipline an employee for false and malicious testimony,[84] nor may an employer initiate a defamation suit against employees for defamatory testimony.[85] The Act protects all employees who participate, not just those 40 years or older,[86] and while the Act speaks only of protecting employees or applicants, former employees are protected from retaliation after they have left that employment.[87]

Opposition

Employees opposing practices made unlawful by the ADEA are protected. Such opposition will be protected even if it is only reasonable to believe that the practice is unlawful.[88]

However, if no reasonable person could find the employer's practice unlawful, opposition to that practice will not be protected.[89]

Conclusion

It has been stated before with regard to other areas of discrimination in employment that librarians are probably as sensitive as any group of employers to the rights of employees. However, librarianship is a field in which, seemingly, few die and none retire and longevity is a norm. It is, therefore, a field that must be particularly alert to the rights of older employees. As we are all inexorably marching toward or have already entered the protected age group, enlightened self-interest suggests we all should pay close attention to the ADEA and its dictates.

Americans with Disabilities Act

The Americans with Disabilities Act (ADA, or the Act) was signed into law July 26, 1990. Congress had found that there were forty-three million Americans with one or more physical or mental disabilities, and that these people were discriminated against in numerous ways, resulting in severe disadvantage socially, economically, vocationally, and educationally. Congress further recognized that the disabled had limited legal recourse against discrimination. As enacted, the ADA provides comprehensive civil rights protection in the areas of employment, public transportation, public accommodations and services operated by private entities, and access to telecommunications. The Act is primarily codified at 42 U.S.C. 12101-12213 with telecommunications at 47 U.S.C. 225 *et seq.* While all areas of the Act are of importance to the disabled, employment and access to buildings, programs, and services are those that impinge on libraries, and it is those areas that are analyzed.[90]

Relationship to Other Acts

The Americans with Disabilities Act is designed to complement and not supersede other acts to curb discrimination against the disabled. The Rehabilitation Act (RA) of 1973 covers federal employees of entities with federal contracts and employees of federal fund recipients. This Act remains in full force, and many of the definitions developed under the RA have been incorporated in the ADA. Many states also have legislation protecting the disabled, and those acts are not superseded by the ADA unless the ADA has more stringent provisions than the state law. In brief, the ADA is the minimum level of protection for the disabled, to which the various states may provide greater protection. Many have done so.

Employment

Under Title I of the Americans with Disabilities Act,[91] the Equal Employment Opportunity Commission (EEOC) has been charged by Congress with the enforcement of the ADA as it relates to employment discrimination. Guidance in interpretation of the employment segment of ADA can be found in the regulations promulgated by EEOC which are found at 29 C.F.R. 1630 ("Regulations") and its appendix.[92]

The employment provisions of ADA became effective July 26, 1992, for employers with twenty-five or more employees employed for twenty or more weeks per year. On July 26, 1994, the minimum number of employees drops to fifteen. Note that the number to count is all of the employees in the organization and not just those in a particular unit. Title II, Subtitle A of the ADA prohibits discrimination on the basis of disability by state and local governments including discrimination in employment. The Department of Justice, which is responsible for the development of regulations to implement Title II, has determined that Congress intended to cover the employment practices of all public entities regardless of size, and thus any library connected with a public entity is subject to the Act.

Undoubtedly, there are private libraries unattached to a larger entity that do not reach the minimum number to be covered, but the vast majority of public, school, academic, and special libraries will be "covered entities" under the ADA.

The ADA does not apply to the federal government, corporations wholly owned by the federal government, Indian tribes, or bona fide private membership clubs exempt from taxation under section 501(c) of the Internal Revenue Code of 1986.

Disability

The ADA prohibits discrimination in employment against a "qualified individual with a disability" because of that disability. To be protected under the ADA, an individual must be both qualified and have a disability.

The term "disability" means, with respect to an individual: (1) a physical or mental impairment that substantially limits one or more of the major life activities of such individual; (2) a record of such impairment; or (3) being regarded as having such an impairment. In order to be found disabled, an individual must satisfy one of these three.

The terms used are not self-defining, and some elucidation is necessary. Physical or mental impairment has no special meaning beyond its plain language understanding, except to note that the disability must rise to a medically recognized condition as opposed to a general physical characteristic.

"Major life activities" are those basic activities that the average person in the general population can perform with little or no difficulty. Major life activities include, among others, caring for oneself, performing manual tasks, walking, seeing, hearing, speaking, breathing, learning, and working.

Through cases brought under the Rehabilitation Act of 1973, the courts have found a number of conditions to be "handicaps," including AIDS, epilepsy, dyslexia, hearing loss, heart disease, and hypertension. There are many other conditions that would qualify as a disability, and it should be noted that the existence of an impairment is to be determined without regard to mitigating measures such as medicines or prosthetic devices.

Certain conditions are specifically excluded from coverage by the Act as not being within the definition of "disabilities." These are homosexuality, bisexuality, transvestitism, transsexualism, pedophilia, exhibitionism, voyeurism, gender identity disorders not resulting from physical impairments, or other sexual behavior disorders. Also excluded are compulsive gambling, kleptomania and pyromania, and psychoactive substance use disorders resulting from current illegal use of drugs. Pregnancy is not considered an impairment and thus is not covered by the ADA. Women are protected against discrimination because of pregnancy under Title VII of the Civil Rights Act of 1964, but this protection does not include the requirement of reasonable accommodation.

Discrimination

The general rule is that no covered entity may discriminate in regard to job application procedures, the hiring, advancement, or discharge of employees, employee compensation, job training, and other terms, conditions, and privileges of employment. As the Act understands the word, discrimination includes:

1. Limiting, segregating, or classifying a job applicant or employee in such a way that adversely affects his or her opportunities or status because of his or her disability. Thus, for example, it would be a violation for an employer to limit the duties of an employee with a disability based on a presumption of what is best for an individual with such a disability. It would be a violation to adopt a separate track for job promotions for employees with disabilities based on a presumption that employees with disabilities are uninterested in, or incapable of, performing particular jobs. Similarly, it would be a violation for an employer to assign or reassign employees with disabilities to one particular office or installation, or to require that employees with disabilities only use particular employer-provided nonwork facilities such as segregated break rooms.

2. Participating in a contractual or other business relationship that has the effect of discrimination against a qualified applicant or employee with a disability. This provision applies to the parties on either side of the contractual or other relationship. For example, an employer may not contract with a third party to test applicants in a way that would be discriminatory if the employer himself did it. Alternatively, an employer who contracts for services from an independent contractor is not without responsibility to the employees of that contractor. The regulations give as an example that an employer who contracts for services to a copier machine would be required to supply, as a reasonable accommodation, a stepstool should the service representative be a dwarf.

3. Discriminating against a qualified individual because that person has a relationship or association with an individual with a disability, for example, not hiring a qualified person because that person's spouse has cancer, out of fear of contagion, that the applicant will be unduly absent, or that it would increase the employer's cost for health insurance. The relationship does not have to be a close personal one. It would be a violation to fire a qualified employee because that employee does volunteer work with people who have AIDS, and the employer fears that the employee may contract the disease.

It should be noted, however, that the employer is under no obligation to provide the applicant or employee without a disability any accommodation because of the disability of the associated person. Thus, for example, an employee would not be entitled to a modified work schedule as an accommodation to enable the employee to care for a spouse with a disability.

4. Not making "reasonable accommodations" to the known physical or mental limitations of an otherwise qualified individual with a disability who is an applicant or employee, unless the employer can show that the accommodation would impose an "undue hardship" on the operation of the business. The Act does not list all those things that constitute reasonable accommodation, but the intent is to provide the otherwise qualified disabled worker with sufficient help to perform the essential functions of the position at a level equal to the performance of a qualified worker without a disability, or to enjoy the same level of benefits and privileges of employment as are available to the similarly situated employee who is not disabled. Included in the things that constitute "reasonable accommodation" are the removal of physical barriers to access, job restructuring, modification of work schedules, acquisition of equipment or modification devices, and the provision of qualified readers or interpreters.

The employer is not required to provide accommodations that might be generally beneficial in everyday living such as a wheelchair or a prosthesis. The accommodation required under the Act is one directly related to the performance of the particular position. Thus, eyeglasses would not normally be a required accommodation, but the employer would be required to provide a visually impaired individual with special magnifying lenses if this would enable an otherwise qualified individual to perform the work and such provision was not an undue burden on the employer. The employer need not opt for the "best" accommodation possible, so long as the selected accommodation is sufficient to meet the job-related needs of the individual being accommodated.

It is obvious that employers are obligated to make reasonable accommodations only for disabilities that are known to the employer. If an employee with a known disability is having difficulty in performing the essential functions of a job, the employer may ask if a reasonable accommodation is needed. As a general rule, however, the burden is on the employee to inform the employer that an accommodation is needed. Determining the appropriate accommodation can be a difficult matter, and ought to be done in consultation with the person to be accommodated. The employer has the right to make the final decision, but if the choice proves to be ineffective, the employer has failed to make a reasonable accommodation and the disabled person has a right of action under the Act. Should the disabled person elect not to accept an accommodation that would make it possible to fulfill the essential functions of a position, that person is simply considered unqualified for the position—and an unqualified person is not protected by the Act.

The term "otherwise qualified" is intended to make clear that the obligation to provide reasonable accommodation is owed only to an individual who, except for the disability, has the necessary experience, skill, education, and/or credentials to perform the job's essential functions. For example, if a library requires applicants to have a degree from an accredited library school and five years relevant experience, it need not provide a hearing impaired applicant any reasonable accommodation if that applicant has not met the stated requirements.

Finally, this provision uses the term "undue hardship" as a condition negating the obligation for the provision of reasonable accommodation. "Undue hardship" is largely but not exclusively an economic question. The term means significant difficulty or expense in, or resulting from, the provision of the accommodation, and takes into account the financial realities of the particular employer. However, the concept is not limited to financial difficulty. "Undue hardship" refers to any accommodation that would be unduly expensive, extensive, or disruptive, or would fundamentally alter the nature or operation of the business. For example, suppose an individual with a disabling visual impairment that makes it extremely difficult to see in dim lighting applies for a position as monitor in a library's microform area and requests that the area be brightly lit as an accommodation. Although the individual might be able to perform the job in bright lighting, the library would probably be able to demonstrate that this particular accommodation, though inexpensive, would impose an undue hardship since the bright lighting would make it particularly difficult for the patrons to read the microforms.

5. Denying employment opportunities simply because such employment would require a reasonable accommodation to be made.

6. Using qualification standards, employment tests, or other selection criteria that screen out or tend to screen out disabled persons unless the standard, test, or other selection criteria are shown to be job related and consistent with business necessity. The employer must, however, provide reasonable accommodation in administering tests.

7. Failing to select and administer employment tests to disabled persons so that the results of the test accurately reflect the abilities of the disabled person rather than the extent of the person's impairment. For example, a written test designed to reveal an applicant's knowledge of reference sources would be inappropriate for an applicant with dyslexia, for the results of the test would tend to show the applicant's difficulty in reading rather than his or her knowledge of the matter asked. However, if reading is an essential function of a position in which no reasonable accommodation can be made, a written test of reading ability would be appropriate.

Medical Examinations and Inquiries

In the preemployment stage an employer may not conduct a medical examination or make inquiries of a job applicant as to whether such applicant is an individual with a disability or as to the nature or severity of any disability. It is also considered discriminatory to ask the applicant about his or her workers' compensation history. The incidence of libraries requiring medical examinations is thought to be exceedingly slim, to say the least, but library employers might utilize medical questionnaires that ask the applicant to list his or her medical history. Such inquiries are viewed as discriminatory under the Act.

An applicant may be asked questions related to the ability to perform job-related functions, but these questions should not be phrased in terms of disability. Thus, a library hiring a driver for the bookmobile may ask if the driver has the proper driver's license and experience, but may not ask whether the applicant has a visual disability.

After an offer of employment has been made and prior to the commencement of employment duties, a medical examination may be required if certain conditions are met. The offer of employment may be conditioned on the results of the examination in certain situations, for example, where the job involves work at great heights and the medical exam uncovers a severe condition of acrophobia. Again, it seems highly unlikely that any library would be in a situation where a preemployment medical examination was necessary. Should the occasion arise, the requisite conditions are (1) that all entering employees are subjected to such examination and (2) that all medical information obtained through the examination be considered confidential and filed in separate medical files.

Illegal Use of Drugs and Alcohol

Unfortunately, libraries are not immune to the problem of employees who use illegal drugs or abuse alcohol. As noted above, individuals currently engaging in the illegal use of drugs are not protected by the ADA. However, an individual who has been successfully rehabilitated and is no longer engaging in the illegal use of drugs, or a person who is participating in a supervised rehabilitation program and no longer engaging in such use may qualify as an individual with a disability.

The library may prohibit the use of drugs and the use of alcohol in the workplace by all employees, may require that employees not be under the influence of alcohol or engaging in the illegal use of drugs in the workplace, and may require drug users or alcoholics to meet the same qualification standards for employment or job performance required of other employees. In other words, neither drug use nor alcohol use, although possibly diagnosed as a disease, is an excuse for unsatisfactory performance.

Other Considerations

1. An employer has a right not to hire an individual who poses a direct threat to the health or safety either to him or herself or to other individuals in the workplace. For example, a library would not be required to hire an individual disabled by narcolepsy (characterized by frequent and unexpected loss of consciousness) for an electrician's job, the essential functions of which involve working with high voltages. In determining whether an individual would pose such a direct threat, the factors to be considered include (1) the duration of the risk; (2) the nature and the severity of the potential harm; (3) the likelihood that the potential harm will occur; and (4) the imminence of the potential harm. Of course, there is always the question of whether the risk can be eliminated or reduced to an acceptable level with reasonable accommodation.

2. Religious organizations may give preference in employment to individuals of a particular religion and may require that all applicants and employees conform to the religious tenets of the organization. However, individuals who meet the religious criteria may not be discriminated against because they are disabled. In other words, the religious entity is required to consider qualified individuals with disabilities who satisfy the permitted religious criteria on an equal basis with qualified individuals without disabilities who similarly satisfy the religious qualifications.

3. Every employer covered under the ADA is required to post notices in accessible formats to applicants and employees describing the applicable provisions of the Act.

Title II: Public Services

The provisions of Title II, subsection A are covered after the discussion of Title III (see p. 69). Title II covers, for entities in the public sector, both employment and access to facilities and programs. The provisions of Title I apply quite uniformly to the employment situations covered in Title II, and many of the considerations of access posed in Title III apply as well. Thus it seems more orderly to discuss Title II after discussion of Titles I and III. It must be emphasized, however, that Title II is not synonymous with Title I or Title III, and attention must be given to the differences. Or perhaps more practically, public entities must pay particular attention to Title II while private entities open to the public should be particularly alert to the demands of Title III.

Title III: Public Accommodations and Services Operated by Private Entities

Title III of the Americans with Disabilities Act[93] prohibits discrimination on the basis of disability by private entities in places of public accommodation and in commercial facilities. The title also prohibits discrimination by any private entity that offers examinations or courses related to applications, licensing, certification, or credentialing for secondary or postsecondary education, professional, or trade purposes.

Private Entity. The term "private entity" is defined as any individual or entity other than a public entity. A public entity is any state or local government and any department, agency, and instrumentality of a state or local government.

Place of Public Accommodation. The regulations define place of public accommodation as a facility operated by a private entity whose operations affect commerce and falls within at least one of twelve listed categories. Those categories generally describe facilities that hold themselves open to the public and invite the public in. Specifically listed is "a museum, library, gallery, or other place of public display or collection."

Disability. Title III understands "disability" to have the same meaning as that described under Employment above.

Requirements

The aim of Title III is to prohibit a public accommodation from discriminating against people with disabilities by denying them the opportunity to benefit from goods or services, by giving them unequal goods or services, or by giving them different or separate goods or services. The result desired is the provision of an equal opportunity for persons with disabilities to partake, through accommodation, the same level of enjoyment in a place of public accommodation as is available to persons without disabilities.

Title III specifically states that it is discriminatory to deny participation, to provide unequal benefits, and to provide separate benefits and that benefits should be provided in the most integrated setting appropriate to the needs of the individual. In order to achieve equality in places of public accommodation, Title III requires public accommodations to modify policies, practices, or procedures where such modification would afford more equal opportunity to disabled persons; to provide auxiliary aids and services; to remove architectural barriers where such removal is readily achievable; and to provide alternatives where barrier removal is not readily achievable.

Modification of Policies, Practices, or Procedures

Every place of public accommodation must modify its policies, practices, or procedures if, by doing so, the modification will allow a person with disabilities more equal access to the goods or services of the entity unless such modification would fundamentally alter the nature of the enterprise. For example, a library with a policy barring vans from the parking lot would have to modify that rule if an individual who uses a wheelchair-accessible van wishes to park in that facility. A library with a policy barring animals would have to modify that policy to permit the use of a service animal by an individual with a disability. Note, however, that the library is not responsible for the care and supervision of the service animal.

The key to meeting the regulations in this area is flexibility. A rigid adherence to set rules is not the avenue to accommodation and it should always be remembered that a foolish consistency is the hobgoblin of little minds.

Auxiliary Aids and Services

The Department of Justice, in interpreting the requirement for the provision of auxiliary aides and services, has determined that such provision applies exclusively to communicative assistance. The regulations list a number of assistive devices for both the visually and hearing impaired, but no particular device is required where communication can be accomplished satisfactorily by some means. For the hearing impaired this may mean use of a notepad and pencil, and for the visually impaired the provision of a person to communicate orally might be sufficient. Obviously, these have their limits and the question arises as to how far an entity has to go in the provision of assistance. The regulations state that such assistance should be provided "unless the public accommodation can demonstrate that taking those steps would fundamentally alter the nature of the goods, services, facilities, privileges, advantages, or accommodations being offered or would result in an undue burden, i.e., significant difficulty or expense" (Regulation 36.303). The particular assistance offered can be a bone of contention, and the best approach is to consult with the disabled person to reach a reasonable accommodation. Clearly, it would be expected that library staff would read card catalog cards to a visually impaired person on a short-term basis; and the organization of volunteers for such purposes should not be difficult or particularly burdensome.

Assistive devices are required to perform or accomplish the central functions of the public accommodation, but are not required for incidental conveniences. Thus, for example, a library that provides a telephone for the incidental convenience of patrons would not be required to provide telecommunication devices for the deaf (TDDs).[94] On the other hand, if telephone reference service is provided, a TDD or some other accommodation would be necessary. Even if not required by the Act, every library should consider all the ways that can enhance the communicative process and have available those that are likely to be useful and are reasonably affordable.

Neither the Act nor the regulations state when the assistance must be available. Clearly, any entity ought to be prepared to meet regularly recurring needs but just as surely, no entity can be expected to have on hand a whole array of devices on the off-chance that someone with a disability needing a particular device will show up. Libraries, of course, are in the business of helping people to use their collections and facilities and should generally face no particular burden under this section. Special programs, association meetings, and the like might pose different problems, however. Announcements of such events should ask for prior notification when special accommodations are desired. The sponsoring agency can then determine whether an accommodation can be made or whether such accommodation is an undue burden for which there is no reasonable substitute. As noted above, the concept of undue burden takes into consideration expense but evidently does not include cost effectiveness. Thus, if an organization can afford a signer for twenty hearing impaired persons it can afford a signer for one hearing impaired person. In any event, the burden is on the disabled individual to identify himself or herself as one in need of auxiliary aids or services.

Removal of Barriers

One of the more obvious ways of increasing access to public accommodations for persons with disabilities is the removal of structural barriers in existing facilities. This is what Title III requires, providing such removal is "readily achievable, i.e., easily accomplishable and able to be carried out without much difficulty or expense."[95] Since the Title deals with public accommodations, it does not extend to areas not intended for public access such as those areas of a facility that are used exclusively as employee work spaces. Such places are, of course, subject to the requirements of Title I, which requires reasonable accommodations for disabled employees although nothing need be done until a disabled person is employed. The regulations list a number of modest measures that may be taken to remove barriers, and that are likely to be readily achievable. The list is illustrative and not exhaustive and includes installing ramps, making curb cuts in sidewalks and entrances, repositioning shelves, repositioning telephones, widening doors, installing accessible door hardware, and removing high pile, low-density carpeting, among others. There are many simple measures that any entity, including libraries, could effectuate making life much easier for the disabled. A period of time spent navigating the library in a wheelchair or blindfolded might be enlightening for any library administrator.

Where alterations are not feasible, entities are expected to provide alternative services or accommodations. Libraries, for instance, are not expected to lower the height of library shelving or widen stack aisles to accommodate wheelchairs; but they are expected to provide an alternate means for a disabled person to retrieve material from those stacks. Title III is careful to point out that public accommodations are not expected to provide personal devices or services to a disabled person; but a distinction is made between providing minor assistance to an individual and providing assistance that substantially does the work of the disabled person. For instance, paging a book from the stacks and filling out a check-out slip for an individual are not services of a personal nature within the meaning of Title III, whereas providing a person to do all the disabled person's research would be beyond reasonable accommodation and not required.

Seating in assembly areas[96] is a matter that could affect libraries with auditoriums or assembly areas. Recall that the Act seeks to integrate the disabled to the greatest degree possible with the general population. Title III seeks to provide seating whereby the disabled, in this case usually in wheelchairs, are not segregated in a special area away from family, friends, and colleagues to the extent possible. The first requirement is to have enough wheelchair seating spaces that, ideally, are dispersed throughout the seating area. If the existing facility makes this impossible, there ought to be movable chairs available for those who wish to sit with the disabled individual in the designated area.

New Construction and Alterations

The Act requires very modest efforts be made in existing facilities to accommodate disabled persons; but the expected efforts for new construction and alterations are considerable. The Act contemplates a high degree of convenient access to ensure that patrons and employees of places of public accommodation and commercial facilities are able to get to, enter, and use the facility.

The ADA is prospective and evolutionary. Its intent is that over time, with new construction and alterations incorporating design to accommodate the disabled, access will become the rule. The Act does not require alterations to be made or new facilities to be constructed. Rather, it patiently awaits the time when necessity dictates alterations or new construction, when the application of design for accommodation for the disabled is not especially burdensome economically. Experience under the Architectural Barriers Act of 1968 and the Rehabilitation Act of 1973, which are models for interpretation of the ADA, has produced some odd results. Both these acts and the ADA require only the portion of the facility actually being renovated to incorporate new design for the disabled. Thus, if toilets are being upgraded, accommodations must be made for wheelchairs. However, there is no requirement to upgrade other access points at the same time unless the area undergoing alteration contains a primary function of the facility, in which case the path of travel to the altered area must be made usable by disabled persons. One can envision the interiors of buildings being wheelchair friendly in many ways and yet the building itself inaccessible because alterations to entrances have not yet become necessary. With time those entrances too will need alterations.

The provisions of the Act regarding new construction applied to facilities designed and constructed for first occupancy after January 26, 1993. This date was applicable only if the final application for a building permit, or extension thereof, was certified as complete after January 26, 1992, or, in jurisdictions that do not certify completion of applications, if the final application or extension thereof was received by the proper authority after January 26, 1992, and if the first certificate of occupancy for the facility was issued after January 26, 1993. These dates were designed to protect those projects that have been long in the process but whose completion, for some reason, has been delayed, from having to make expensive alterations not considered necessary when the facility was planned. A facility not meeting these dates is treated by the Act as an existing facility.

The Act, and the rules developed to implement it, both require new construction to be "readily accessible and usable by individuals with disabilities." This phrase, with minor modifications, has been used in the Architectural Barriers Act of 1968, the Fair Housing Act, the Rehabilitation Act of 1973, and now in the current accessibility standards. The phrase means that a facility can be approached, entered, and used by individuals with disabilities (including mobility, sensory, and cognitive impairments) easily and conveniently. The Department of Justice has adopted the Americans with Disabilities Act Accessibility Guidelines (ADAAG) and facilities constructed or altered in accordance with these guidelines or the Uniform Federal Accessibility Standards (UFAS), developed under the Architectural Barriers Act, will be considered readily accessible. The ADAAG and UFAS have very similar provisions, word for word in some instances, and both have sections covering special criteria for libraries, making it difficult to recommend one standard over the other. One might reasonably assume, however, that the ADAAG would be preferred, as that set of guidelines was specifically adopted by the Department of Justice for implementation of Title III.

The regulations for new construction contain several exemptions, only two of which appear likely to affect libraries. One is structural impracticability. The requirement that a new construction be accessible does not apply where an entity can demonstrate that it is structurally impracticable to meet the requirements of the regulation. This exemption assumes that the terrain is such that no economically feasible way of providing accessibility is possible. Such a condition will undoubtedly be extremely rare.

The Act also provides for an "elevator exemption" for certain buildings. An elevator is certainly the best way to provide access for the disabled to floors above and below the entry level. Congress determined, however, to exempt facilities with fewer than three stories regardless of the square footage of the stories and any facility regardless of the number of stories where each story has less than 3,000 square feet. If the library should be a part of a shopping mall the exemption would not apply. Note very carefully, however, that entities covered by Title II of the ADA, that is, state and local governments and their instrumentalities, do not qualify for the elevator exemption (Regulation 35.151). Public, school, state university, and other governmental libraries are, of course, covered by Title II.

Alterations

Title III of the ADA requires that alterations to a public accommodation begun or in progress after January 26, 1992, must be built so as to ensure that, to the maximum extent feasible, the altered part of the facility is readily accessible to, and usable by, individuals with disabilities. An alteration, as the word suggests, is a change to a place of public accommodation that affects, or could affect, the usability of the facility. An alteration does not include normal maintenance, reroofing, painting, or cosmetic changes.

In general, alterations must conform with the ADAAG, although the phrase "to the maximum extent possible" reflects an understanding that the existing facility may make complete compliance with ADAAG impossible. Entities that are exempt from elevator requirements for new construction are also exempt under alterations. It was noted above that alterations to an area of a facility that contains a primary function require, to the maximum extent feasible, that the path of travel to the primary area be made readily accessible. The regulations provide that this requirement cannot be evaded by performing a series of smaller alterations if those alterations could have been performed as a single undertaking.

Public Services

Title II Subtitle A of the ADA extends the protection afforded by section 504 of the Rehabilitation Act of 1973 (which covers all programs receiving federal financial assistance) to all public entities whether or not they receive federal funds. "Public entities" includes any state and local government and any of their departments, agencies, or other instrumentalities. Public libraries, and any library attached to a state entity, obviously fall within this group.

To a very large degree, the protections afforded by Titles I and III of the ADA are the protections provided by Title II. Title II speaks of discrimination in not allowing the disabled participation in the services, programs, or activities of a public entity, but this is analogous to Title III's prohibition in denying goods and services to persons with disabilities. While much that has been discussed above in connection with Title I (employment) and Title III (public accommodations and commercial facilities) applies to the entities covered by Title II, there are some significant differences. These include:

Self-Evaluation. Every public entity is required to evaluate its current services, policies, and practices to see that they do not interfere with the requirements of Title II. In doing so, the public entity must allow interested persons an opportunity to participate in the self-evaluation by submitting comments. Where the self-evaluation identifies necessary modifications, the entity should proceed to make them. The self-evaluation must have been completed by January 26, 1993, but note that Title II became effective on January 26, 1992, and any liabilities arising under Title II are not shielded by this requirement.

Any public entity that employs fifty or more persons must maintain for three years after the evaluation a file containing:

1. A list of the interested persons consulted,

2. A description of the areas examined and any problems identified, and

3. A description of any modifications made.

Any entity that made such an evaluation in compliance with section 504 of the Rehabilitation Act of 1973 needed only to evaluate those policies and practices not included in the previous self-evaluation.

Notice. Every entity must provide to applicants, participants, beneficiaries, and other interested persons information regarding the entity's provisions for implementing procedures which assure compliance with the Act, and to apprise such persons of their rights and protections assured them by the Act. No particular form of notice is required.

Designation of Responsible Employee. Institutions employing fifty or more persons must appoint an individual to coordinate efforts to comply with the Act, and to handle complaints arising under the Act. The entity must also adopt and publish grievance procedures that provide for prompt and equitable resolution of complaints.

Perhaps the most significant difference between Titles II and III lies in the area of "program accessibility." Unlike Title III of the Act, which requires public accommodations to remove architectural barriers where such removal is "readily achievable" or to provide goods and services through methods that are "readily achievable," Title II requires a public entity to make its program accessible in all cases except where to do so would result in a fundamental alteration in the nature of the program or in undue financial or administrative burdens. The Department of Justice has determined that Congress intended the "undue burden" standard in Title II to be significantly higher than the "readily achievable" standard in Title III; and the regulations expect that the program access requirement of Title II would enable individuals with disabilities to participate in and benefit from the services, programs, or activities of public entities in all but the most unusual cases.

In order to comply with the strictures of Title II, a public entity such as a public library is not required to make each of its existing facilities accessible to and usable by individuals with disabilities. Thus, it would be sufficient, in a system with branch libraries, that one of the branches or the main library be accessible to disabled individuals.

Where structural changes are required to comply with the obligations established by the Act such changes should be accomplished promptly, but in any event, no later than January 26, 1995. Institutions with fifty or more employees that had to make structural changes must have developed, within six months of January 26, 1992, a transitional plan setting forth the steps necessary to complete such changes. The institution must provide an opportunity for interested persons and groups to participate in the development of the transitional plan by submitting comments.

Miscellaneous Provisions

Title V provides a number of provisions that affect the implementation of the ADA. In addition to provisions included in the discussion above, what this title provides, among others, is not directly applicable to libraries:

- that a state shall not be immune under the eleventh amendment from legal action for violation of the Act;
- a prohibition against retaliation against anyone for opposing discrimination under the Act;
- that in any action taken under the Act, the court may allow the prevailing party, other than the United States, a resonable attorney's fee, including litigation expenses, and costs, and the United States shall be liable for such expenses the same as a private individual;
- where appropriate and to the extent authorized by law, the use of alternative means of dispute resolution, including settlement negotiations, conciliation, facilitation, mediation, factfinding, minitrials, and arbitration, is encouraged to resolve disputes arising under the Act.

Other Provisions of the ADA

Aside from those provisions discussed above that effect libraries, the ADA has two other titles not likely to impinge on library operations. Title II Subtitle B covers public transportation and Title IV deals with telecommunications.

NOTES

1. Laffey v. Northwest Airlines, Inc., 185 App DC 322, 567 F.2d 429 (1976).

2. 29 C.F.R. 800.150 (1985).

3. Corning Glass Works v. Brennan, 417 U.S. 188 (1974).

4. 560 F.2d 12 (1977).

5. Named from the case Coleman v. Jiffy June Farms, Inc., 458 F.2d 1139 (1971).

6. 469 U.S. 111 (1985).

7. McLaughlin v. Richland Shoe Co. 486 U.S. 120 (1988).

8. See 29 U.S.C.S. 216(b), 216(c), 217 and 29 C.F.R. 1620.33.

9. 29 U.S.C.S. 216(b).

10. Codified at 42 U.S.C.S. 2000e *et seq.*

11. 2000e(e)(2).

12. Ansonia Board of Education v. Philbrook, 479 U.S. 60 (1986).

13. 432 U.S. 63 (1977).

14. 29 C.F.R. 1605.2(e).

15. 42 U.S.C.S. 2000e-1

16. 483 U.S. 327 (1987). The entity involved was a gymnasium owned by the Mormon church. Amos, a custodian, was fired because he was not a member of the church. The Supreme Court upheld the coverage of the exception to nonprofit entities of the church with the suggestion that for-profit entities would be treated differently.

17. 29 C.F.R. 1604.1 et seq.

18. See Earnhardt v. Puerto Rico, 582 F.Supp. 25 (1983).

19. 29 C.F.R. 1606.7.

20. 411 U.S. 792 (1973).

21. 401 U.S. 424 (1971).

22. Walls v. Mississippi State Dept. of Public Welfare, 730 F.2d 608 (1983); Townsend v. Nassau County Medical Center, 558 F.2d 117 (1977); Rice v. St. Louis, 607 F.2d 791 (1979); EEOC v. Georgia Pacific Corp., 450 F.Supp. 1227 (1977); Merwine v. Board of Trustees, 754 F.2d 631 (1985).

23. See, e.g., Hawkins v. Anheuser-Busch, Inc., 697 F.2d 810 (1983).

24. 42 U.S.C.S. 2000e-5(g) as amended by the Civil Rights Act of 1991.

25. 42 U.S.C.S. 2000e-5(k) as amended by the Civil Rights Act of 1991.

26. Reeb v. Economic Opportunity Atlanta, Inc., 516 F.2d 924 (1975).

27. EEOC v. University of Detroit, 701 F.Supp. 1326 (1988). In Delaware State College v. Ricks, 449 U.S. 250 (1980), the court found the date of notification of the termination began the period within which to file. The difference between the cases was that in Ricks the notice was final while in the Detroit case the parties were still negotiating between the time of notification and the actual termination.

28. Bazemore v. Friday, 478 U.S. 385 (1986).

29. Roberts v. Gadsden Memorial Hospital, 850 F.2d 1549 (1988).

30. Williams v. Saxbe, 413 F.Supp. 654 (1976).

31. 29 C.F.R. section 1604.11.

32. Meritor Savings Bank v. Vinson, 477 U.S. 57 (1986).

33. 58 Federal Register 51266, October 1, 1993. As these rules make clear, just plain gender baiting can constitute sexual harassment, but in almost all cases there is harassment of a sexual nature exacerbated by the prsence of nonsexual hostile conduct.

34. Neville v. Taft Broadcasting Co., 857 F.2d 1461 (1987).

35. See, for example, Chamberlain v. 101 Realty, 915 F.2d 777 (1990).

36. There is some argument that the two sexes have differing standards and that with a female plaintiff, the standard ought to be that of the "reasonable woman." For a full discussion of the issue see Lindemann and Kadue, *Sexual Harassment in Employment Law* (Washington, DC: Bureau of National Affairs, 1992), pp. 181–84. That argument aside, it should be noted that both the rules cited in footnote 33 above and in the Supreme Court's latest ruling on sexual harassment, Harris v. Forklift Systems, Inc., 62 LW 4004, decided November 9, 1993, use the reasonable person standard.

37. 477 U.S. 57, at 58 (1986).

38. Swentek v. USAir, Inc., 830 F.2d 552 (1987).

39. Phillips v. Smalley Maintenance Services, Inc., 711 F.2d 1524 (1983).

40. See, e.g., Keppler v. Hinsdale Township High School Dist., 715 F.Supp. 862 (1989); also Evans v. Mail Handlers, 32 F.E.P. 634 (1983).

41. Williams v. Civiletti, 487 F.Supp. 1387 (1980).

42. 29 C.F.R. 1604.11(a)(3).

43. Walter v. KFGO Radio, 518 F.Supp. 1309 (1981).

44. Hall v. Gus Construction Co., 842 F.2d 1010 (1988).

45. Henson v. Dundee, 682 F.2d 897 (1982).

46. Morgan v. Hertz, 725 F.2d 1070 (1981).

47. Reed v. Shepard, 939 F.2d 484 (1991).

48. Meritor Savings Bank, FSB v. Vinson, 477 U.S. 57 (1986).

49. Miller v. Aluminum Co. of America, 679 F.Supp. 495 (1988).

50. EEOC Dec. 85-9, 37 FEP Cas 1839 (1985).

51. EEOC v. Sage Realty Corp., 507 F.Supp. 599 (1981).

52. Sardigal v. St. Louis Nat. Stockyards Co., 42 FEP Cas 479 (1986).

53. EEOC Dec. 81-17, 27 FEP Cas 1791 (1981).

54. Bennett v. Corroon & Black Corp., 845 F.2d 104 (1988). The plaintiff collected nothing, however, as the corporation was very decent to her trying to make every accommodation and continuing to pay her on a leave of absence she took because of the incident. There was simply no relief left for the court to award her.

55. Arnold v. City of Seminole, Okl., 614 F.Supp. 853 (1985).

56. 760 F.Supp. 1486 (1991).

57. 42 U.S.C.S. section 2000e(b).

58. 29 C.F.R. section 1604.11(c).

59. 833 F.2d 1406 (1987).

60. See, for example, Tunis v. Corning Glass Works, 747 F.Supp. 951 (1990) (pictures were removed immediately; Hirschfield v. New Mexico Corrections Dept., 916 F.2d 572 [1990] [plaintiff interviewed at lunchtime, alleged perpetrator placed on administrative leave by evening].

61. Robinson v. Jacksonville Shipyards, Inc., 760 F.Supp. 1486, at 1518.

62. 29 C.F.R. 1604.11(f).

63. The determination of qualifications of an employer under ADEA is bor-

rowed directly from Title VII cases. Thurber v. Jack Reilly's, Inc., 717 F.2d 633 (1983) is typical and states the matter well.

64. E.g., Minker v. Baltimore Annual Conference of United Methodist Church, 699 F.Supp. 954 (1988); Cochran v. St. Louis Preparatory Seminary, 717 F.Supp. 1413 (1989).

65. See EEOC v. Manchester East Catholic Regional School Bd., 430 F.Supp. 188 (1977); Ritter v. Mt. St. Mary's College, 496 F.Supp. 724 (1980).

66. Chapman v. Detroit, 808 F.2d 459 (1986).

67. Jones v. Janesville, 488 F.Supp. 795 (1980).

68. Howard v. Daiichiya-Love's Bakery, Inc., 714 F.Supp. 1108 (1989).

69. See 29 C.F.R. 1626.8.

70. Oscar Mayer v. Evans, 411 U.S. 750 (1979).

71. Incredibly, this actually happened. In Hodgson v. First Fed. Savings & Loan Ass'n. of Broward County, Fla., 455 F.2d 818 (1972) the interviewer did write "too old" on the interview form, and in Naton v. Bank of Cal., 647 F.2d 691 (1981) the interviewer noted the interviewee was "over the hill."

72. J. E. Kalet, *Age Discrimination in Employment Law* (Washington, DC: Bureau of National Affairs, 1986) p. 59.

73. Haskell v. Kaman Corp., 743 F.2d 113, at 121 (1984).

74. 411 U.S. 792 (1973).

75. 450 U.S. 248 (1981).

76. 29 C.F.R. 1625.6(b).

77. Arritt v. Grisell, 567 F.2d 1267 (1977) upheld a maximum beginning hiring age of 35 for municipal police officers and EEOC v. Missouri State Highway Patrol, 748 F.2d 447 (1984) upheld a maximum beginning age of 32 for highway patrol radio operators, but Hahn v. Buffalo, 770 F.2d 12 (1985) found a maximum beginning age of 29 for police officers invalid under the ADEA.

78. 29 U.S.C.S. section 626(b).

79. Loeb v. Textron, Inc., 600 F.2d 1003 (1979).

80. See Spagnuolo v. Whirlpool, 717 F.2d 114 (1983); cf., Lander v. Lujan, 888 F.2d 153 (1989).

81. Monroe v. United Airlines, Inc., 32 BNA FEP cas 1259 (1983).

82. The cases are numerous. See annotation "Award of 'Front Pay' under §7 of Age Discrimination in Employement Act of 1967," 74 ALR Fed. 745 (1985) and its pocket part (1993).

83. 29 U.S.C.S. section 623(d).

84. Pettway v. American Cast Iron Pipe Co., 411 F.2d 998 (1969).

85. Buzogany v. Roller Bearing Co., 47 BNA FEP Cas 1485 (1988).

86. Anderson v. Phillips Petroleum Co., 722 F.Supp. 688 (1989).

87. Passer v. American Chemical Soc., 935 F.2d 322 (1991).

88. Jennings v. Tinley Park Community Consol. School Dist. No. 146, 864 F.2d 1368 (1988).

89. Holden v. Owens-Illinois, 793 F.2d 745 (1986).

90. In the Rehabilitation Act of 1973 Congress used the term "handicaps" when referring to physical or mental impairments. In ADA congress preferred the term disabilities as the most current terminology. The terms are considered substantively equivalent by the EEOC.

91. 42 U.S.C.S. 12111-12117.

92. A widely available publication issued by the EEOC and the U.S. Department of Justice in October 1991 is the *Americans with Disabilities Handbook*, which contains the law and the regulations.

93. 42 U.S.C.S. 12181-12189.

94. The term "text telephone" seems to be increasingly preferred, as the disability requiring the device may be a speech (not a hearing) disability.

95. Regulation 36.304.

96. Regulation 36.308.

3

EMPLOYMENT SECURITY

Employment is necessary for the individual to earn a living. Employment also provides the individual with a sense of self-worth and a particular niche in society. In short, one's job is the defining element of one's position in society, perhaps supplanting one's relation to land ownership of earlier years. Over the centuries the duties owed to each other by the employee and the employer have differed, but the question is constant: What degree of loyalty is owed between the parties and how is this expressed?

The question has overtones of morality, with perhaps some sociological implications, but the answer is grounded in economics. The best system is that which is most productive or most profitable. There are certain humanitarian constraints within which the economic system is supposed to work and laws abound to impose these, but, at bottom, approaches to employment are measured by productivity and profitability.

There are many employment theories, but it is probably true that there is no natural antipathy between management and labor. Some views of the best way to induce productivity and profitability quite naturally cause an antipathy between employer and employee, however. Industrial relations in the nineteenth century caused a tremendous amount of labor strife where standard thought was for the employer to get the most out of, and give the least to, the employee. It was a contest of raw power, of which the individual employee had little. The courts and legislatures did little to redress this imbalance until well into the twentieth century.

In the 1930s, the federal government began addressing this imbalance of power through legislation protecting unionization. Unionization had, and has, the effect of protecting the employee, but it does not address the question of productivity. Current management theory embraces the concept of employee involvement in management and decision making. This is an interesting approach to both productivity and employee satisfaction, but there is potential for conflict toward the adversarial system of unions and management; certainly there seems to be potential (if not already a fact) for conflict with the laws protecting unionization. The sections that follow discuss the present state of employment protection that exists under certain conditions.

Employment-at-Will

Employment-at-will simply means that both the employer and the employee can terminate an employment relationship at any time, for any reason, or for no reason, unless there is a valid agreement in place to the contrary. On its face, the rule seems equitable in that both parties have the right to terminate employment, but in fact it is not. Few employers are harmed by the departure of an employee; but most employees are placed in a critical position with the loss of a job. The concept of employment-at-will took hold at the latter part of the nineteenth century in the United States, and received the blessing of the U.S. Supreme Court in cases that struck down legislation seeking to limit the right of employers to fire at will.[1] The Court took the position that such legislation was an unconstitutional infringement of the employer's liberty of contract.[2] The Court occasionally upheld legislation regulating employment in particularly hazardous conditions, but essentially clung to the substantive due process position until the late 1930s, when it abandoned the approach altogether.[3] This shift left the door open for the states to modify, either legislatively or judicially, the employment-at-will doctrine, but not all states chose to do so. At present ten states, Delaware, Florida, Georgia, Iowa, Louisiana, Mississippi, Missouri, North Carolina, Rhode Island, and Utah, remain strong employment-at-will states. The others recognize, in greater or lesser degree, some one or more modifications to the doctrine.[4]

The employment-at-will doctrine applies to private sector employers and their nonunion employees. The rights of public employees are extensively regulated by statute. The law concerning the discharge of public employees will generally be found in those statutes. Public employees also have constitutional rights not available to private sector employees. Job protection and employee benefits for union members are governed by the collective bargaining agreements entered into. These areas are discussed below.

Exceptions to the Employment-at-Will Doctrine

Exceptions to employment-at-will are usually categorized under the rubrics of public policy, implied promises, and implied covenants of good faith and fair dealing. Each of these have various subcategories.

Public Policy Exceptions

Terminations in Violation of Statutes. Various statutes such as the Equal Pay Act, Title VII, the Age Discrimination in Employment Act, and others designed to protect employee's rights, uniformly have provisions against employer retaliation for exercising those rights. For example, it would be illegal to terminate the employment of one who has filed charges of sexual harassment or one who has filed complaints about minimum wages or overtime.

Whistleblower Protection. Many jurisdictions will protect an informant from termination when he or she has reported illegal activities by the employer, although the approach is far from uniform. Some states have statutes protecting whistleblowers while in others the enforcement is judicial. The statutes may differ greatly from state to state. Rhode Island, for instance, has a whistleblower statute protecting public employees but not private employees unless their employer does $200,000 or more of annual business with state or local government.[5] Michigan, on the other hand, covers both public and private employers and defines an employer as a person who has one or more employees that provides pretty complete coverage.[6]

Whistleblower protection doesn't require the whistleblower to report illegal activity to governmental authority. Protection has been given to employees who have tried to induce the employer to conform with laws and regulations. In almost all cases, however, the complaint must deal with a specific illegal activity. Protection will not be afforded an employee who makes general complaints about the "unethical" nature of the employer's business[7] or who makes general statements about the safety of the employer's product.[8]

Public Policy Exception. The definition of public policy is not easily encompassed. The concept generally includes those things guaranteed by the Constitution and sometimes those things protected by statute and judicial decision. However, as one court put it, "More often . . . it abides only in the customs and conventions of the people—in their clear consciousness and conviction of what is naturally and inherently just and right between man and man."[9] In short, public policy says that it isn't right to fire a person for attempting to do something that is legally required. For example, the courts of California protected an employee of a labor union who was fired for refusing to perjure himself before a legislative committee, which would have been a criminal act.[10] The courts of Maryland protected the employment of an apartment manager who refused to commit the civil offense of trespass (a tort) by entering apartments without permission.[11] In states that recognize public policy, most courts will protect an employee who is fired for fulfilling a civic duty such as voting, doing jury duty, or testifying in court. However, the courts quite uniformly require a clear mandate of public policy. For example, courts will not recognize internal disagreements as to accounting and management practices[12] or ideological differences concerning the prosecution of cases,[13] for these do not constitute public policy and thus do not constitute an exception to the employment-at-will rule.

Implied Contract Exceptions

In the past several decades, courts have begun to recognize various promises concerning termination of employment made by employers as valid contracts between employee and employer. Often they take form in an employee's handbook where a statement such as "employees will be fired for just and sufficient cause only" or "tenure is assured as long as the employee is productive except for acts of moral turpitude" will be an enforceable contract. Such promises may also be in other forms such as in letters offering employment, or they may be oral.

Oral promises pose particular problems but they are nevertheless enforceable in the right circumstances. The obvious problem is in proving the promise was made and also that the words were uttered seriously and that it was reasonable for the employee to rely on them. Less well known to the general public is the Statute of Frauds, which most of the states have adopted, based originally on the English law passed in 1676. The Statute of Frauds requires, among other things, that any contract not to be performed within a year must be in writing. Thus an oral contract for three years is unenforceable, as contrary to the Statute of Frauds. However, an oral contract for life would, in most states, be enforceable because the employee's life may end within the year. The majority rule is that the test for whether the Statute of Frauds applies is what could have happened when the contract was entered into, not what, in fact, did happen. So, the contract that was valid remains valid even after the employee survives the year. Don't try to make any sense of it, just be aware that there is a Statute of Frauds (except in Louisiana, Maryland, and New Mexico) and its application varies.[14]

Oral promises, or conditions in conjunction with written promises or conditions, may also run afoul of the "parol evidence rule," which says that previous oral agreements are understood to merge in the written contract and a written contract cannot be altered by subsequent parol evidence. Parol evidence can, however, be used to clarify the meaning of a written contract if the evidence is not contradictory.

One pesky problem with implied contracts that promise certain conditions of employment is modification of the promise at some time after the employee begins employment. The courts generally take the view that employers have the right to make modifications in the various conditions of employment, and somehow it seems right, but it is difficult to find a contract theory to fit the circumstance. Any unilateral modification on the part of the employer would seem a blatant breach of contract. Some courts take the view that modification is an offer of a new contract by the employer and a continuation of work is acceptance of the offer by the employee.[15] In *Toussaint v. Blue Cross and Blue Shield of Michigan*, the Supreme Court of Michigan simply held that employer statements of policy can give rise to contractual rights in employees "although the statement of policy is signed by neither party, can be unilaterally amended by the employer without notice to the employee, and contains no reference to a specific employee, his job description or compensation, and although no reference was made to the policy statement in pre-employment interviews and the employee does not learn of its existence until after his hiring."[16] No rationale here, just a statement of policy.

Modifications to implied contracts should not be uniformly viewed as detrimental to employees. Quite the opposite, in fact, may be the case. Employers often upgrade benefits and institute procedures for the better operation of the enterprise, presumably in the expectation of maintaining a stable and productive workforce. In cases concerned with modification, the question often is whether a premodification employee has the right to enjoy the benefits of the modification. As the cases cited show, the employee frequently wins. However, employees should take note of an alarming trend in health care coverage where employers are moving from traditional group health care plans to self-insured plans. The Employee Retirement Income Security Act (ERISA) provides little regulation of self-insured plans, but in the name of uniformity, the act bars states from regulating such plans. The courts tend to treat these plans as merely one more benefit subject to unilateral modification which can leave the employee with little coverage for specific illnesses.[17] It would be sound policy, in any event, for every employer who issues a handbook, or otherwise promulgates policy concerning employment conditions, to indicate that that policy may be modified unilaterally at any time in the future.

Implied Covenant of Good Faith and Fair Dealing

Section 205 of the *Restatement (Second) of Contracts* states, "Every contract imposes upon each party a duty of good faith and fair dealing in its performance and its enforcement."[18] This statement applies to contracts generally. A few states have taken the spirit of the statement and applied it to termination of employment cases. *Fortune v. National Cash Register Co.*[19] is usually cited as the leading case in this area. Fortune was a salesman working under a written contract that specifically recognized that the employment could be terminated at will upon written notice. The employment was terminated, as it happened, just prior to the time Fortune was in a position to earn a large commission. *Fortune* thus stands for the proposition that, in Massachusetts, an employee may not be terminated for a reason that amounts to bad faith and unfair dealing. In *Cleary v. American Airlines, Inc.*,[20] a 1980 case, California extended this principle to mean that all dismissals must be for just cause. Cleary had been employed for eighteen years and the court evidently felt that such longevity deserved to be terminated only where there was legal cause. Subsequently the California courts have construed *Cleary* to imply a covenant of good faith and fair dealing only when there is longevity of employment involved or the employer has promulgated a policy for adjudicating employee disputes.[21] In *Foley v. Interactive Data Corp.*[22] the Supreme Court of California again recognized the covenant of good faith and fair dealing but limited recovery under it to contract remedies. The Nevada Supreme Court upheld a finding of a tortious bad faith discharge in violation of an implied covenant of good faith and fair dealing because contract damages would be insufficient to punish the employer who, in this case, dismissed an employee to avoid paying retirement benefits.[23]

The distinction between a public policy exception and a covenant of good faith and fair dealing exception to the employment-at-will doctrine is not great. A situation could fall within either depending on the particular court. In broad terms, the public policy exception requires a policy that affects the public generally. It is not sufficient that it be a policy the public generally approves of; rather it must be a policy that impinges upon all of society in theory, if not in fact. A covenant of good faith and fair dealing, on the other hand, involves only the individual in question. Thus, it would affect important public functions if employees were threatened with being fired for testifying in court; but it would affect only the individual were he or she fired just prior to becoming eligible for retirement benefits. The public policy exception would protect in the first instance but not in the second. The covenant thus can be a useful tool, although few states have chosen to use it.

Public Sector Employment
Constitutional Protections

Individuals employed by the government are afforded rights in their employment, guaranteed by the Constitution, that are not available to individuals employed in the private sector. The First Amendment to the United States Constitution protects, among other things, the freedom of speech and religion. The Fifth Amendment provides, in part, that no person shall "be deprived of life, liberty, or property, without due process of law, ..." The Fourteenth Amendment states:

> No State shall make or enforce any law which shall abridge the privileges or immunities of citizens of the United States; nor shall any State deprive any person of life, liberty, or property, without due process of law; nor deny to any person within its jurisdiction the equal protection of the laws.

Initially, the Bill of Rights (the first ten amendments) applied only to the federal government, while the Fourteenth Amendment, by its language, applies to the states. Through a process known as incorporation, the Fourteenth Amendment has made most of the provisions of the Bill of Rights applicable to the states. The Supreme Court has interpreted the clause in the Fifth Amendment quoted above to encompass the concept of "equal protection"[24] with the result that cases on both the federal and state level present a relatively seamless understanding of the law.

The common statutory avenue for implementing the Fourteenth Amendment against state officials is 42 U.S.C.S. 1983, which states:

Every person who, under color of any statute, ordinance, regulation, custom, or usage, of any State or Territory, subjects, or causes to be subjected, any citizen of the United States or other persons within the jurisdiction thereof to the deprivation of any rights, privileges or immunities secured by the Constitution and laws, shall be liable to the person injured in an action at law, suit in equity, or other proper proceedings for redress.

Unfortunately, except for the lawyers, the wording of section 1983 is less than self-evident. The upshot, however, is that cases brought under either the Fourteenth Amendment or 1983 must meet the requirement of "state action." In brief, the Fourteenth Amendment says that "No State" will deprive or deny the people, as stated above, and 1983 requires that action be "under color of" state laws, among others. One looks, therefore, for the "state nexus" that triggers the "state action." It should be noted that the word "state" includes all levels of government and not just the state per se.

In most cases the question of whether the state is involved is not difficult. Most branches of government are readily recognized: police and fire departments, schools, public universities, and a variety of public agencies are clearly departments of the state; any action by such departments constitutes "state action." For many so-called public libraries, however, the answer isn't simple, although it is probable that most institutions that consider themselves private probably are as a matter of law.

The case that probably most closely parallels the quasipublic library situation is *Rendall-Baker v. Kohn*[25] wherein a private school for problem students undertook the education of special students under contract with towns that had a state mandated requirement to educate such students. The school received up to ninety-nine percent of its funding from public funds, its curriculum was state mandated, and its hiring of staff was reviewable by the State Committee on Criminal Justice. When staff were fired, a suit was brought alleging violation of the First, Fifth, and Fourteenth Amendments. The essential question here is whether there is the necessary state action to invoke the constitutional protections or section 1983. The Court found that the school operated essentially as a contractor, and while the state controlled many aspects of the contract, it did not interfere in personnel decisions such as firing staff. The dissent by Justice Marshall seems to be more soundly reasoned, but the fact is, the Supreme Court is not quick to find state action unless there is present an individual or agency with a clear state connection somehow present and exercising a significant degree of control.

In New England particularly but elsewhere also, there are institutions that call themselves "The [Somewhere] Public Library." These institutions would seem to be agencies of the government in that they perform a public function, are usually supported to some extent by public funds, and may be to some degree under the direction of the local government, but these libraries have independent boards of trustees and make operational decisions independent of the government. Under Supreme Court precedents, they are not state agencies and their actions are not "state action." On the other hand, those libraries whose boards of trustees are appointed by governmental officials, or elected by the public, would probably be considered to have sufficient "state nexus" that their actions would be considered state action for purposes of invoking either the Fourteenth Amendment or section 1983. The question becomes easier when the library is supported out of municipal funds and the building is owned by the community, but the central question remains: Is the government sufficiently involved that the actions of the institution can be understood to be actions of the government?

The Rights Guaranteed

Assuming that state action can be found, certain rights flow to the individual. Both the Fifth and Fourteenth Amendments promise equal protection and due process of the law. These concepts are critical to the protection of rights.

Equal Protection

On its face, the term "equal protection" would seem to imply that all persons within the jurisdiction of the United States will enjoy equally the bounty controlled by the government. This obviously is not the case because, for example, not everyone is eligible for food stamps. What equal protection is really concerned with is classifications. The government classifies groups of people all the time to determine benefits and privileges, and equal protection comes into play to determine whether the classification meets constitutional standards.

In order to determine what standards apply, the courts have fashioned categories that trigger different levels of response. First, there are "suspect" categories that will trigger "Strict Scrutiny," that is, the courts will closely analyze the classification to see whether it is designed to achieve some compelling state interest and also whether the classification is as narrowly drawn as possible. Classification by race is always suspect; alienage and national origin usually are as well. If any classification impinges on a "fundamental" right, that also will give rise to strict scrutiny. What rights are fundamental is not completely clear but presumably included are most of those guaranteed by the Constitution and the various amendments. The Court has specifically ruled that the right to vote and to travel and the right of privacy in marriage are fundamental rights.

A second tier of classifications deemed "suspicious" will invoke heightened scrutiny whereby the state will have to prove that the classification serves an important state objective and is not so inherently invidious as to trigger strict scrutiny. Gender and illegitimacy fall within this group.

Finally, classifications that disadvantage or favor particular groups, neither suspect nor suspicious, will be upheld if there is some (any will do) rational relation between the classification and some valid governmental function.

Equal protection covers much more than employment, of course. However, in the employment sphere it is an important concept.

Due Process

The phrase "due process" sounds simple enough, but has in fact engendered reams of controversy. The words give the impression that the matter is merely concerned with proper procedure. While procedure is a part of it, it is much more. The phrase applies to what the government can do; and it implies that the government must conduct itself with fairness and in a reasonable way. Due process means that the state must do the right thing as doing the right thing is understood.

While the extent and precise meaning of the term "due process" are continually under debate, there is some consensus on the core meaning of the phrase. There is agreement that there are two types of "due process," one of which is substantive due process and the other procedural due process. Substantive due process looks to see whether the substance of a particular law, rule, or regulation offends the constitution, for example, whether a regulation barring employees from wearing campaign buttons is permissible. Procedural due process looks to see whether the government has taken the proper steps in taking a particular action. As a practical matter, substantive due process no longer looms very large in the court calendar because its issues have been subsumed under other rubrics; procedural due process, however, retains much vitality.

Procedural due process begs the question "what process is due?" As suggested above, the heart of the matter is to reach a fair resolution of the problem presented. It is agreed to a point beyond dispute that a fair procedure requires notice to the individual involved of the nature of the action intended, that the individual involved has a right to a hearing before an impartial body, and that the individual has a right to a determination that is impartially derived from the facts presented. Beyond this there is dispute as to what other procedures are due. There are questions of when a hearing is due, for example, before or after termination, whether the individual has the right to counsel, whether the hearing is adversarial with cross-examination of witnesses, whether the individual has the power to subpoena witnesses, and any number of other problems. In the employment arena, procedural due process is extremely important even if limited to the basic considerations. Simply put, public employees cannot be summarily fired. They do have substantial protections against arbitrary decisions.

Specific Protections

Public employees generally have all the protections of the various civil rights laws discussed elsewhere in this work. Why, then, look for constitutional protections? The answer to that is (1) it may be more advantageous to follow the constitutional route because greater recovery may be possible and the statute of limitations may be more favorable, and (2) the statutes are quite specific in what they cover; it may be that a particular grievance, not covered by statute, could be adjudicated under section 1983.

Collective Bargaining

Another approach to employment security is unionization and collective bargaining. Professional librarians have debated the question of whether unions are appropriate at the professional level, with no firm conclusion. The model for unions is an employee-employer relationship in the industrial context, where dispute resolution rests finally on economic considerations, a model not especially apt for libraries where the work is not measured in economic outcomes. However, the same was said of collective bargaining in the public sector some twenty-five years ago, and public sector collective bargaining has increased markedly in terms of percentage of potential coverage, while unionization has decreased in the private sector in terms of potential coverage. It is a fact, regardless of philosophical positions, that librarianship is not a heavily unionized field at the professional level. Where the librarians are unionized it is generally because the library is part of a larger entity in which professionals are unionized, for example, in a university where there is a faculty union. Clerical and other subprofessional workers are much more likely to be unionized than are professionals in all types of libraries. As there are professional unions, the matter is not without interest to librarians generally.

The first problem presented in a discussion of collective bargaining is the lack of uniformity between public sector and private sector collective bargaining. The private sector is covered by federal legislation that very largely has preempted state control, either legislative or judicial, in this area, and that provides a nationwide uniformity to collective bargaining. There is no parallel federal legislation covering public sector collective bargaining, which means there are fifty separate approaches to the matter, a different one for each state. It is true that many states have modeled their legislation for public sector collective bargaining on the federal plan covering the private sector, and decisions by the National Labor Relations Board are persuasive with state labor boards and courts. For libraries in the private sector a grasp of the federal legislation is essential, and for libraries in the public sector such knowledge could be useful, although a knowledge of one's own state laws is an absolute necessity in this area.

Private Sector Collective Bargaining

The Wagner Act[26]

The National Labor Relations Act of 1935, generally called the Wagner Act after its leading proponent, Senator Robert Wagner of New York, was the first piece of federal legislation to promote the development of unions and collective bargaining. The act declared that workers have the right to organize and to bargain collectively, and lists five employer unfair labor practices. Specifically, it is an unfair labor practice for an employer to

1. interfere with, restrain, or coerce employees in the exercise of their rights to organize, bargain collectively, and engage in other concerted activities for their mutual aid or protection
2. dominate or interfere with the formation or administration of any labor organization or contribute financial or other support to it
3. encourage or discourage membership in any labor organization by discrimination with regard to hiring or tenure or conditions of employment
4. discharge or otherwise discriminate against an employee because he has filed charges or given testimony under the act
5. refuse to bargain collectively with the representatives of his employees

The act established the National Labor Relations Board (NLRB, or Board) whose function is to administer the act and to make determinations on unfair labor practices. The Act included no restrictions on union activity.

The Taft-Hartley Act

Unions thrived under the Wagner Act to a point where it was perceived (by a Republican Congress, at least) that labor had too much power and thus some balance was needed. In 1947 Congress passed, over President Truman's veto, the Taft-Hartley Act (officially the Labor-Management Relations Act), the heart of which was to set up unfair labor practices on the part of unions. The Act is an amendment to the Wagner Act and retained the five unfair labor practices of employers. The major unfair labor practices of unions are

1. to restrain or coerce employees in the exercise of their rights guaranteed by the Act
2. to restrain or coerce an employer in the selection of his bargaining or grievance representative
3. to cause or attempt to cause an employer to discriminate against an employee on account of his membership or non-membership in a labor organization

4. to refuse to bargain in good faith with an employer

5. to induce or cause employees to stop work in order to force employer or self-employed person to stop doing business with another person (secondary boycott)

6. to induce or encourage employees to stop work in order to force an employer to assign work to members of a particular union instead of to members of another union (jurisdictional strike)

7. to cause or attempt to cause an employer to pay for services not performed (featherbedding)

Along with the additions to the list of unfair labor practices, the Taft-Hartley Act also narrowed union security devices. The closed shop, which obligates an employer to hire only union members, was outlawed. Under the Act, unions and employers may negotiate a union or agency shop whereby employees must join the union, or along with the agency shop pay the equivalent of union dues within a specified period of time. However, the Act specifically allows states to pass so-called right-to-work legislation, which, where passed, forbids union membership or dues as a requirement of employment. Since the NLRB requires the union to represent all employees whether they are union members or not, the net result of right-to-work laws is to allow some employees a free ride.

The Act expanded the NLRB from three to five members and established the office of General Counsel, whose major task was and is to handle the Board's unfair labor practice prosecutorial functions. Finally, the Act makes collective bargaining agreements enforceable in federal district court and provides a civil damage remedy to private parties injured by secondary boycotts. The Taft-Hartley amendments to the Wagner Act succeeded in turning a federal pro-labor policy into a neutral policy that still preserved the right to unionize and bargain collectively.

The Landrum-Griffin Act

In the late 1950s the McClellan Committee of the U.S. Senate investigated wrongdoing on the part of unions, which resulted in passage of the Labor-Management Reporting and Disclosure Act (the Landrum-Griffin Act)[27] in 1959. While the act made some amendments to the NLRA, its major purpose was and is to protect the rights of union members. It contains a bill of rights protecting members' equal rights, freedom of speech and assembly, the right to sue, and other safeguards. The act requires certain financial disclosures by unions, prescribes rules and guidelines for electing union officials, regulates "trusteeships" (a procedure where a national or international union could take over a subordinate union for good reasons, often resulting, however, in raids on the local union's treasury and suspension of the rights of local officials), establishes a fiduciary responsibility for officers of unions, and provides civil and criminal penalties for financial abuses perpetrated by union officials. The Secretary of Labor is made the watchdog of union conduct with powers to investigate and prosecute violations of the Act.

The amendments to the NLRA contained in the Landrum-Griffin Act are not the sort likely to affect libraries. For example, bargaining for "hot cargo" clauses in a contract is forbidden. (Hot cargo is material produced by an employer with whom the union has a dispute; such clauses would allow employees to refrain from handling that material, thereby effectively barring the union's own employer from doing business with the other employer.) One important amendment that might very well affect libraries gives state courts and state labor relations boards jurisdiction over cases rejected by the NLRB under its jurisdictional standards.

NLRB Jurisdiction

The jurisdiction of the Board under the Act is extremely broad. The commerce clause of the United States Constitution gives Congress the right to regulate interstate commerce, and the Act applies to all employees of employers who are engaged in enterprises that "affect commerce" and covers all labor disputes that "affect commerce." As with other acts that rely on the commerce clause, the operation can be somewhat removed from actually doing business interstate and still be considered to be doing business that affects commerce. A library, for instance, that buys books and materials exclusively from in-state wholesalers is affecting commerce if the wholesaler buys materials from another state.

Under the statute the NLRB has two major functions. One is to oversee the process of forming unions, which includes the determination of appropriate bargaining units and who may belong to those units and overseeing the actual process of electing the representative body. The other is to investigate and adjudicate unfair labor practices. Although the NLRB has the power to regulate every employer engaged in operations affecting commerce, it limits itself to covering those enterprises that affect commerce substantially. Under what are called "jurisdictional standards," the Board has set dollar amounts for particular types of enterprises. For example, a private university or college must have at least $1 million in gross annual revenue from all sources excluding certain restricted donations; a taxicab company must do $500,000 worth of business; law firms and legal assistance programs must have at least $250,000 in gross annual revenues.[28] If an enterprise should fail to meet the minimum, it would have recourse to state courts and labor boards as provided by the 1959 amendments.

In addition to the jurisdictional standards that restrict coverage, the Act itself eliminates large areas of coverage simply by definition. As noted, the Act covers employees of employers whose enterprises affect commerce. However, by definition, the Act does not consider the United States or any state government, any political subdivision of either, any government corporation or federal reserve bank, or any employer subject to the Railway Labor Act to be an employer. The result, of course, is that such entities are not covered by the NLRA. Employers and employees not covered by the Act may, of course, form and recognize unions but such unions will not be certified by the NLRB nor will any regulations be enforced by the NLRB.

The Bargaining Unit

The Act provides employees the right to self-organization and freedom of choice, but it vests in the NLRB the authority to determine whether a unit chosen is "appropriate" for the particular group of employees who wish to organize. The Board has broad authority to determine whether a unit is appropriate, and looks to such factors as community of interest among employees, whether they comprise a homogeneous and distinct group, whether they are interchanged with other employees, the extent of common supervision, previous history of bargaining, and geographic proximity of various parts of the employer's operation to determine that a unit is appropriate. Thus, for example, it would be appropriate to have a unit of professional librarians, but it would also be appropriate for academic librarians to be included in a faculty bargaining unit. In one case library assistants were excluded from a unit of custodial and maintenance employees because they were clerical employees with a separate community of interest, but library aides and messenger clerks were found to perform essentially manual tasks and could be included in such a unit.[29] Beyond determining that the unit is appropriate is the question whether the union the unit wishes to affiliate with is appropriate. In fact, the only concern is whether the union is willing to take on the task of bargaining for the unit, and unions such as the Teamsters and the United Auto Workers often represent library support staff.

Aside from the question of whether a unit is appropriate for certain classes of employees, the Act and Board policy restrict certain types of employees from belonging to a bargaining unit, the Act simply declares certain groups and types not to be "employees" and therefore not covered by the Act. Employees who are determined not to be employees under the Act include agricultural workers, domestic servants, individuals employed by their parents or spouses, independent contractors, supervisors, and individuals employed by an employer subject to the Railway Labor Act. Also excluded from coverage are employees considered "managerial" and "confidential," as their interests are thought to coincide more closely with the employer than the bargaining unit.

Special considerations attach to certain designated employees. Professional employees may not belong to a bargaining unit made up of nonprofessional workers unless a majority of the professional workers vote for inclusion in such unit, under the theory that professionals would normally be outnumbered and their concerns outweighed by the interests of production workers, a matter not particularly applicable to libraries. Guards may not be included in a unit with other, nonguard employees on the theory that those whose job it is to protect the property of the employer should not be put in a position where loyalties may be divided. Occasionally a problem arises in determining whether the duties of such employees as janitors involve guard duties, but the cases suggest that the guard duties have to be fairly substantial. Merely locking up at night will not suffice.

Managerial Employees

By policy of the NLRB, managerial employees are excluded from coverage of the Act. Managerial employees are those individuals who participate in the formulation of policy and provide meaningful input in the decision making process. In *Yeshiva* the Supreme Court found that the faculty were managers and thus excluded from forming a union under the Act. The Court stated:

> The controlling consideration in this case is that the faculty of Yeshiva University exercise authority which in any other context unquestionably would be managerial. Their authority in academic matters is absolute. They decide what courses will be offered, when they will be scheduled, and to whom they will be taught. They debate and determine teaching methods, grading policies, and matriculation standards. They effectively decide which students will be admitted, retained, and graduated. On occasion their views have determined the size of the student body, the tuition to be charged, and the location of a school. When one considers the function of a university, it is difficult to imagine decisions more managerial than these. To the extent the industrial analogy applies, the faculty determines within each school the product to be produced, the terms upon which it will be offered, and the customers who will be served.[30]

This raises a serious question as to whether professional librarians are managers. Academic librarians who align themselves with teaching faculty will be measured along the *Yeshiva* lines. Other librarians, regardless of the type of library, would seem to be the proper subject for managerial analysis, but in fact the Board tends to view the work of librarians, with the exception of the head librarian, who would be considered a manager in most cases, ministerial rather than managerial. New approaches to management involving collective decision making such as participative management suggest that the Board might take a new look at managerial positions, but that has not materialized. So far, the Board has tended to analyze such arrangements to determine whether participants are supervisors, who, like managers, may not belong to a bargaining unit.

Supervisors

The Act specifically bars supervisors from being members of bargaining units on the belief that such persons would have loyalties more aligned with the employer than with the bargaining unit, thereby causing a conflict of interest. Supervisors are employees who have authority over other employees in significant ways. Authority to hire, fire, or suspend fellow employees or to make effective recommendations that such action be taken is evidence that the individual is a supervisor. Other indicia are independent authority to discipline, reward, promote, and schedule working conditions or adjust grievances of employees.[31]

If an individual exercises any supervisory control over another member of a bargaining unit, that supervisory person is barred from representation in the unit. If, however, a person supervises nonunit employees, the Board takes the position that that person should not be barred from representation in a unit of employees whose principal duties are of the same character as his or hers because of sporadic supervisory authority over nonunit employees. *Adelphi University*,[32] in dealing with this matter, stated that "where professionals regularly (more than fifty percent of their time) supervised nonunit employees"[33] they would be excluded. Later cases hardened this fifty percent line into the sole criterion for determining whether a supervisor of nonunit employees was a supervisor in terms of the Act. However, the NLRB has recently repudiated this. "We reject any such shorthand approach. Rather, to ascertain whether an individual's exercise of supervisory authority over employees outside the unit warrants his exclusion as a supervisor, we must make a complete examination of all the factors present to determine the nature of the individual's alliance with management."[34] Undoubtedly anyone spending more than fifty percent of his or her time in supervising nonunit employees will be found a supervisor, but as the Board determined in *Detroit College of Business*, one can spend a good deal less than fifty percent of one's time in such supervisory activity and still be a supervisor.

Another viewpoint on the matter was presented in *New York University*,[35] where the Board noted the relative imprecision of the supervisory question in professional employee settings. Professional employees, the Board pointed out:

> frequently require the ancillary services of nonprofessional employees in order to carry out their professional, not supervisory, responsibilities. But that does not change the nature of their work from professional to supervisory, nor their relation to management. They are not hired as supervisors but as professionals. The work of employees that may be "supervised" by professionals in this category is merely adjunct to that of the professional and is not the primary work product.[36]

This is not contrary to the finding in *Detroit College of Business*. Rather, it presents a particular factor to be analyzed in the process of determining supervisory personnel. It is an approach particularly suitable to libraries, in which professionals are hired to do professional work, not to supervise employees who actually produce the end product. Under this analysis most professional librarians would not be found to be supervisors.

Evidently participatory management schemes will not result in finding librarians as supervisors either. Such arrangements utilize committees or teams (and inevitably there is a committee chair or a team leader), and the question is whether that individual is a supervisor. In a case closely analogous to participatory management in libraries, Anamag, a Carrollton, Kentucky, company, utilized a managerial philosophy referred to as a "team concept." Production employees were arrayed in teams and each team had a team leader elected by members of the team. The question, of course, was whether the team leader was a supervisor. In *Anamag*[37] the Board found that the team did make significant decisions but that the leader had no independent authority over other employees to implement management's policies. This would seem to square with many participatory schemes adopted by libraries where decisions are arrived at collegially and no one is in a position of authority, in terms of supervisory authority under the Act, on the team or committee.

The Organization Process

The process in which a union is organized is fairly straightforward and clear-cut. The proper procedures are laid out and the Board stands ready to oversee the process. The Act has put forward various procedures considered unfair labor practices for both the employer and the union organizers, and the Board will adjudicate those on proper appeal.

The first step in establishing a union is to determine whether there is sufficient interest among the employees. Organizers establish what they think is an appropriate unit and attempt to gather authorization signatures. Thirty percent in favor of a union is considered a sufficient interest to call for an NLRB election. If a dispute arises concerning any of a number of factors, such as whether the unit is appropriate or whether certain persons may properly be a part of the unit, the Regional Director of the NLRB field office will first attempt to resolve the issue(s) informally, but if this is unsuccessful, he will hold a hearing and make a determination. These determinations are appealable to the Board in Washington unless the parties consent to abide by the Regional Director's decision. The Board's determinations are generally not reviewable unless the employees can show that the Board decision was contrary to provisions of the Act, the so-called "Kyne" exception, wherein the appropriate Federal District Court will take jurisdiction.[38] The Kyne exception is not ordinarily applicable to employers because employers can refuse to bargain with the union certified as a result of representational proceedings. Such refusal would cause unfair labor practice charges, which would secure Court of Appeals review of any NLRB order resulting from an unfair labor practices proceeding in which the employer's objection to representation proceedings can be raised.[39]

Between the time a date is set for the election and the election itself, both employer and union may and usually do campaign for or against a vote for the union. Such campaigns are circumscribed by various proscriptions, that is, unfair labor practices, in the Act itself and by NLRB interpretations of the Act. Unfair labor practices by employers were listed in the discussion of the Wagner Act, but those are subject to interpretation of which the Board has provided many. The following indicate the types of activity prohibited to both employer and union, although it must be noted that in the development stage the vast majority of unfair labor practices appear to be on the part of employers attempting to discourage unionization.

Statements. Generally, either side can make statements of opinion about unions and can provide information as long as they are not coercive and do not contain threats or promises. At one time the Board would review election propaganda to see whether misleading statements were sufficient to invalidate an election, but that is no longer the case. However, the line between misleading statements and threatening statements is very thin and the Board will find the latter a violation of the Act.

Surveillance. In and of itself surveillance is not an unfair labor practice, but if it has the effect of intimidation so as to skew one's acceptance or rejection of the union it will be a violation.

Interrogation. Interrogation concerning union matters will usually be found to be coercive, although isolated instances of questioning are generally insufficient to cause a violation. The question is whether the questioning is intimidating or threatening, which may be determined by circumstances such as who is doing the questioning, where it is being done, and by what means. Questioning by the company president in his office of a production worker seldom off the production floor probably would be a violation, as would questioning in an employee's home by company officials. Tape recording the questioning session, using court stenographers to record proceedings, and questioning about union activity during a polygraph test would all undoubtedly be unfair labor practices, but questioning by a supervisor who is a friend and social companion would probably not be.

Polls. There are many legitimate reasons for conducting a poll, such as determining the strength of support for a union, but as in all these activities, the question is whether the activity is done in such a way as to be intimidating, threatening, or coercive. A poll that provides absolute anonymity for those polled would probably be all right, but asking for a show of hands of those who favor a union in a meeting in which company officials indicated a dislike for unions would surely be an unfair labor practice. Polling by unions is generally permissible.

No-solicitation rules. Many employers have rules barring solicitation of any kind on their premises. If such rules are enforced generally, they may be enforced against union solicitation, particularly if the ban is on solicitation during working hours. Prohibition of union solicitation during nonworking hours, such as breaks and mealtime, however, will generally be found violative of the Act.

Union organizers who are nonemployees generally have a right to access to employees on property of the employer, subject to reasonable rules such as access in designated areas during nonworking hours. No-access rules will usually be an unfair labor practice.

Interference with wearing union insignia. A ban on union buttons has been uniformly found to be an unfair labor practice absent some factor necessitating the ban for reasons of plant discipline or safety. While many cases mention plant discipline, no examples are offered as to how buttons affect discipline. Safety is actually seldom affected by buttons and other insignia, although it is often put forward as the reason for the ban.

Changes in employment terms. Employers have the right to change employment terms, to increase fringe benefits, to give bonuses and the like as they see fit, unless such act has the intent or result of discouraging organizational activity. Benefits conferred just before a representation election would probably constitute an unfair labor practice, and benefits conferred only on those identified as anti-union would surely be such, but the Board will generally look to the totality of circumstances for its determination. For instance, past practices of the employer might indicate a pattern of giving bonuses at certain times or in certain conditions, the financial condition of the employer might suggest the purpose of the benefit, and the record of the employer as antagonistic or not toward unions might suggest whether the benefit was given in good faith.

Discharges and layoffs. Employers generally have the right, subject to various restrictions discussed above under employment-at-will, to select and retain a workforce of their choosing, except that they may not make personnel decisions that impede or coerce employees in their right of self-organization and representation. Dismissal for any valid reason such as incompetence or violation of company rules is not an unfair labor practice unless the action is applied discriminatorily against employees active in unionization, that is, where the same level of incompetence or the same infraction of rules is tolerated in those known to be anti-union and not in those known to be pro-union.

Some activities are strictly in the province of union action or, at least, are more likely to pertain to union activity. These include:

Organizational picketing. Section 158 (b) (7) makes such picketing unlawful in three specific situations: (1) where another union has recognition rights which cannot be challenged; (2) where there was a valid election in the past twelve months; and (3) where no election petition has been filed within a reasonable time, that is, thirty days. Absent these three conditions organizational picketing is permitted.

Violence and threats of violence. Violence or threats of violence on the part of either employer or employee in connection with organization would be an unfair labor practice, but the Act, in section 158 (b) (1) (A), speaks specifically to labor unions in barring violence by the union against employees.

Economic inducements. In connection with organization, unions may not offer any of a variety of economic benefits to persons who join the union such as free life insurance or union jackets. Waver of initiation fees, however, is generally not seen as an unfair labor practice.

The Election

Once disagreements are ironed out, the Regional Director of the NLRB field office will order an election. The Director has the authority to determine the time and place of voting. Usually, the place will be the place of employment, but it doesn't have to be and the time is set to allow all employees in the unit a chance to vote. Any union that can show that it has signed up one employee has a right to be on the ballot. The contest, then, is between the union or unions and no union. If no single option has a majority the two top vote getters have a run-off election.

Certification

If a union receives a majority of votes, the Board will certify it as the sole bargaining agent for the unit. If a no-union vote is in the majority, the Board will issue a certificate of the results of the election, which acts as a bar to another union seeking recognition for one year. Certification requires both parties to bargain in good faith and places on the union the particular duty of fair representation for all its members. If a contract is signed, the contract will act as a bar to rival unions' seeking recognition during the period of the contract for a period of time up to three years, the so-called contract-bar rule.

Two other points might be noted in connection with certification. One is that under certain conditions where the employer has engaged in such unfair labor practices as to foreclose the possibility of conducting a fair election, the Board may certify the union on the basis of authorization cards alone provided the union can show a majority of employees have signed them. The other is decertification. Employees may wish to be rid of their union and a petition for an election may be filed by a union, an employee, or a group of employees, although not by an employer or supervisor. As with the certification process, thirty percent or more of the employees must support the petition. The contract-bar rule and other Board rules affect a decertification election just as they do a representation election.

The Contract

The Act makes it mandatory for both union and employer to bargain in good faith over "wages, hours, and other terms and conditions of employment."[40] While almost anything of possible interest to either party might be seen to impinge, however remotely, on terms and conditions of employment, the Board and the Courts have found a number of things that do not directly affect wages, hours, and other terms and conditions of employment that are considered voluntary subjects of negotiation. Finally, there is the category of illegal subjects.

Mandatory subjects include the obvious areas of salary and wages, hours, vacations, sick leave, health insurance, pension plans, promotion procedures, tenure and sabbaticals in academic institutions, union security and dues checkoff, grievance procedures and arbitration, and no strike/no lockout clauses. Indeed, almost anything providing or removing a benefit in connection with employment is mandatory. For example, the right to hunt on company land, which the employees had had for twenty years, was found to be a mandatory subject for bargaining.[41] Subjects deemed to be mandatory must be bargained for in good faith by both parties to the point of impasse. Failure to do so is an unfair labor practice.

Nonmandatory or voluntary subjects include those things of interest to one or both parties but not actually part of the employment. Such matters would include a clause requiring a secret ballot in voting on the contract, the elimination of a minor benefit unused by most employees, or an agreement as to the size of the bargaining team. Either party can propose a voluntary subject, and if both sides agree, the matter can be included in the contract. However, if there is opposition to the proposal, there is no obligation on the opposing party to bargain on the issue at all, and failure to bargain on the issue is not an unfair labor practice. On the other hand, if a party insists on the inclusion of a voluntary subject without which he won't approve the contract, that is an unfair labor practice.

Illegal subjects are those things forbidden by the Act to be included in a contract, such as a "hot cargo" clause or provision for a closed shop. Such subjects may not be a part of the contract even if both parties agree to the issue.

Strikes

The Act preserves the right of employees to strike, and the strike remains the final weapon in any private sector union's arsenal. A strike action is fraught with danger for the employee, for not only is salary in jeopardy, but the job itself may be lost; witness the PATCO strike in 1981 and the Caterpillar strike in 1991. The Board classifies strikes into types, which determine the degree of protection the strikers have. The types are unfair labor practices strikes, economic strikes, and unprotected strikes.

Unfair labor practice strikes. As the name suggests, these strikes are in protest of unfair labor practices of the employer. The employer may not permanently replace the striking employee, and upon an unconditional offer to return to work, the striking employee is entitled to his or her job notwithstanding the presence of a replacement worker. That individual may have a cause of action against the employer for breach of contract, depending on the promises made during hiring, but the striking employee has the old job back.

Economic strikes. Included in this category are strikes for better wages and working conditions and also those strikes involved in union recognition or organization. Economic strikers have some protection but not a great deal. They may be permanently replaced but they remain employees who, upon unconditional request for reinstatement, are entitled to their jobs should the replacement leave, unless the striking employee has obtained a job substantially equal to the old job.[42] If the striking employee whose job is lost to a replacement should apply as a new hire, the employer may not discriminate against that person for the union activity. Also the employer is barred from discriminating against returning strikers by giving replacements "super-seniority."[43]

Unprotected strikes. This category includes strikes barred by law and those contrary to a valid contract. Strikers in this category are not protected from discharge by the employer, may be permanently replaced, and have no right to reinstatement. Persons involved in a legitimate strike may become unprotected through certain actions taken in connection with the strike. For example, a picketer who called customers who crossed the picket line obscene names lost her protection,[44] and strikers who engaged in violence against nonstrikers lost their protection.[45]

In any discussion of strikes, two things, at least, ought to be noted. The first is that strikes are not the natural outcome of collective bargaining and one would be in error to assume that unions and collective bargaining mean that strikes are inevitable. In fact, the great majority of collective bargaining agreements are made without resort to the strike. The second point is that a strike is not fatal to one's job security. Besides the protections noted above for strikers, there is the fact that any employer is best served by a stable, productive workforce. If an employer has such a workforce and those people go on strike, the costs of replacements in terms of training and productivity are considerable, and the ultimate result might well be a workforce no less militant than the original group of workers.

Conclusion

The National Labor Relations Act as amended has provided a national framework for the development of union activity in the private sector. It is a system designed for an industrial environment in which accommodations are reached in light, ultimately, of economic power. There is an assumption underlying the scheme that labor and management are antagonistic and adversarial, and this undoubtedly remains true in some industries; however, we may be in a managerial revolution in which both labor and management realize that more is to be gained through cooperation than confrontation. Certainly libraries, with their move toward participative management and collegial decision making, need to move away from any adversarial mode of conducting business. It is certainly true that not very many libraries are in a situation in which the

NLRA applies, but it is also true that the NLRA as interpreted by the NLRB and the courts provides the paradigm for union activity in the public as well as the private sector.

Public Sector Collective Bargaining

As noted at the beginning of this section, there is no uniform approach to collective bargaining in the public sector. There is no NLRA to provide unity for unions in the public sector, and the upshot is that each state treats the matter in its own way. It is impossible, therefore, to put forward a general statement about collective bargaining in the public sector. There simply is no general rule. Anyone interested in the matter must look to the particular state in which he or she resides to see how the matter of collective bargaining is handled. Over forty states do have legislation dealing with collective bargaining by public entities, but each tends to handle the matter in its own way. What needs to be done is to look to one's own state to determine the following: what statutes cover public unions, who may unionize, what procedures must be followed to gain recognition and certification, what parameters exist for determining a proper bargaining unit and who may belong to that unit, what is the proper subject matter of collective bargaining, what are unfair labor practices, and who has jurisdiction over the process. The matter is not hard to uncover. Check the state laws annotated and the appropriate sections of digests of legal opinions and consult with the labor department every state has.

The one thread that quite uniformly runs through the legislation is that unions of public employees do not have the right to strike. This has brought forward the importance of alternative dispute resolution, particularly arbitration, and the public employee unions may be testing and proving avenues that will be useful to unions in the private sector.

NOTES

1. See Adair v. United States, 208 U.S. 161 (1908) and Coppage v. Kansas, 236 U.S. 1 (1915).

2. This approach to the law falls under the rubric of substantive due process, an approach that made the enactment of progressive legislation covering hours, wages, and working conditions difficult to say the least.

3. In two key cases, West Coast Hotel v. Parrish, 300 U.S. 379 (1937) and National Labor Relations Board v. Jones and Laughlin Steel Corporation, 301 U.S. 1 (1937), the Court, perhaps alerted to the political and economic tenor of the times by Roosevelt's attempt to "pack" the court, upheld hours and wages law and the constitutionality of National Labor Relations Act. This shift is noted by nearly every commentator as "the switch in time that saved nine." And so I join them.

4. Steven M. Sack, *The Employee Rights Handbook* (New York: Facts on File, 1991), pp. 113–18.

5. R.I.G.L. 36-15-1, *et seq.*

6. M.C.L. 15.361, *et seq.*

7. Pierce v. Ortho Pharmaceutical Corp., 84 N.J. 58, 417 A.2d 505 (1980).

8. Geary v. United States Steel Corp., 456 Pa. 171, 319 A.2d 174 (1974).

9. Payne v. Rosendaal, 147 Vt. 488, 520 A.2d 586, 588-89 (1986).

10. Peterman v. International Brotherhood of Teamsters, 174 Cal. App.2d 184, 344 P.2d 25 (1959).

11. Kessler v. Equity Management, Inc., 82 Md.App. 577, 572 A.2d 1144 (1988).

12. Suchodolski v. Michigan Consolidated Gas Co., 316 N.W.2d 710 (1982).

13. Newman v. Legal Services Corp., 628 F.Supp. 535 (1986).

14. For a very useful elucidation see Henry H. Perritt, Jr., *Employee Dismissal Law and Practice* (New York: John Wiley & Sons, 1987), pp. 219–21.

15. See Pine River State Bank v. Mettille, 333 N.W.2d 622, at 627 (1983) and Helle v. Landmark, Inc., 472 N.E.2d 765, at 775 (1984).

16. 292 N.W.2d 880, at 892 (1980).

17. See "Now You're Insured, Now You're Not," an op-ed piece by Thomas B. Stoddard. *New York Times*, May 23, 1992, p. 23. The case in point is McGann v. H & H Music Company, 946 F.2d 401 (1991). The Supreme Court denied certiorary.

18. Restatement (Second) of Contracts (1979).

19. 373 Mass. 96, 364 N.E.2d 1251 (1977).

20. 111 Cal. App.3d 443, 168 Cal Rptr. 722 (1980).

21. See Shapiro v. Wells Fargo Realty Advisors, 152 Cal. App.3d 467, 199 Cal Rptr. 613 (1984).

22. 254 Cal. Rptr. 211, 47 Cal. 3rd 697 (1988).

23. K Mart Corp. v. Ponsock, 732 P.2d 1364 (1987). This brings up a matter that is generally beyond the scope of this work but a brief explanation of contract and tort damages might be helpful here. Under contract, law damages are compensatory or nominal but not punitive. In the employment sphere this means that an employee can get only those things he or she would have got had there been no breach of contract, e.g., back pay, seniority, and reinstatement but nothing that looks like a windfall. Under tort theory, a plaintiff can collect not only compensatory but also punitive damages that normally are limited only by the jury's or the court's generosity.

24. Bolling v. Sharpe, 347 U.S. 497 (1954).

25. 457 U.S. 830 (1982).

26. The National Labor Relations Act and its amendments, which come largely from the Taft-Hartley and Landrum-Griffin Acts, are codified at 29 U.S.C.S. sections 141–187.

27. Except for the sections amending the NLRA, the Landrum-Griffin Act is codified at 29 U.S.C.S. sections 401–531.

28. The standards are listed in U.S. NLRB. *A Guide to Basic Law and Procedures under the National Labor Relations Act* (Washington, DC: Government Printing Office, 1991), pp. 43–45.

29. President and Directors, Georgetown College for Georgetown University, 200 NLRB 215, 82 LRRM 1046 (1972).

30. NLRB v. Yeshiva University, 444 U.S. 672 (1980).

31. NLRB v. First Union Management Corp., 777 F.2d 330 (1985).

32. 195 NLRB 639, 79 LRRM 1545 (1972).

33. Id. at 644.

34. Detroit College of Business, 296 NLRB no. 40, 132 LRRM 1081 (1989).

35. 221 NLRB 1148, 91 LRRM 1165 (1975).

36. Id. at 1156.

37. 284 NLRB 621, 125 LRRM 1287 (1987).

38. Boire v. Greyhound Corp., 376 U.S. 473 (1964); Leedom v. Kyne, 358 U.S. 184 (1958).

39. Leedom v. International Brotherhood of Electrical Workers, 278 F.2d 237 (1960).

40. 29 U.S.C.S. 158 (a) (5) and 158 (d).

41. Southland Paper Mills, Inc. 161 NLRB 1077, 63 LRRM 1386 (1966).

42. Laidlaw Corp., v. NLRB, 414 F.2d 99 (1969).

43. NLRB v. Erie Resister Corp., 373 U.S. 221 (1963).

44. Montgomery Ward & Co. v. NLRB, 374 F.2d 606 (1967).

45. Oneita Knitting Mills v. NLRB, 375 F.2d 385 (1967).

4

PRIVACY IN THE WORKPLACE

Privacy is a fundamental right constitutionally protected in some of its forms, although the word is not mentioned in the Constitution. Broadly, the term covers two areas that are not particularly closely related. One is the right to be left alone, and the other is autonomy over oneself. The first category includes the right to be free from intrusion on one's solitude, the right not to have one's character shown in a false light, the right to keep the details of one's life from public disclosure, and the right not to have one's likeness used for commercial purposes. Autonomy over oneself includes, as of this writing, a woman's absolute right to an abortion during the first trimester, the right to use contraceptive devices, the right of married couples, and in many states, consenting adults, to indulge in sexual practices of their choice, the right to choose or reject medical treatment, the right to refuse life-support systems, and the right to commit suicide. This last is a right that cannot be taken away although aiding and abetting suicide is often a criminal act. Ironically, in fifteenth-century England attempted suicide was a capital crime that would seem to assure the desired result.

Privacy has a special place in the American psyche, and it is a right most Americans hold as dear as any other. In deciding the landmark case *Griswold v. Connecticut*, Justice Douglas found a penumbra emanating from the First, Third, Fourth, Fifth, and Ninth Amendments that embodied the concept.[1] Alan Westin, in his classic *Privacy and Freedom*,[2] has put forward the value of privacy to the individual: it allows the development of personal autonomy; it permits emotional release from the pressures imposed by societal roles; it provides emotional space for self-evaluation; and it allows for control over communication one has with the rest of society. In short, it allows the individual to develop as an individual. Professor Edward Bloustein some years ago stated the case in singular, albeit slightly sexist, terms:

The man who is compelled to live every minute of his life among others and whose every need, thought, desire, fancy or gratification is subject to public scrutiny, has been deprived of his individuality and human dignity. Such an individual merges with the mass. His opinions, being public, tend never to be different; his aspirations, being known, tend always to be conventionally accepted ones; his feelings, being openly exhibited, tend to lose their quality of unique personal warmth and become the feelings of every man. Such a being, although sentient, is fungible; he is not an individual.[3]

It seems unlikely that the average person thinks of his or her privacy in these terms; rather, each person thinks only that certain things are nobody else's business and is uneasy that certain things might become known that they prefer not be known.

Of the two broad areas of privacy, only the right to be left alone impinges on libraries in a legal way. One can imagine, of course, a situation in which a library patron, somehow obviously suicidal, seeks and is refused information on how best to do the deed. The legal question presented here is whether the library has the right to refuse to provide information if, in fact, it has that information available. And it is not at all farfetched to imagine a governmental edict banning publicly supported libraries from the dissemination of abortion information, but so far, these situations have not come to pass and so will not be discussed here. Thus, the areas of privacy discussed below are limited to the subjects of patron confidentiality in use of library materials and privacy of employees in the workplace.

Patron Confidentiality

It is the goal of every library to provide patrons with the best possible information, and libraries constantly strive to eliminate any barrier that may deter access to or use of materials that a patron may think has useful information. One such barrier to the free and uninhibited use of materials is the fear that knowledge of the use of certain materials suggests something unfavorable about the user of those materials. Over the years there have been a number of incidents in which law enforcement personnel have searched library records for borrowers who had an interest in subjects related to crimes under investigation. At first blush it may seem creative police work to identify possible suspects in this way, but the fact is it casts a pall of suspicion on individuals showing interest in a particular subject matter, and the showing of that interest is not sufficient probable cause for investigation. From the library point of view, however, the problem is that such an approach by authorities makes the patron apprehensive in the use of certain materials. The American Library Association has had a policy on the confidentiality of library records since 1971 (revised in 1975) and the Code of Ethics (1981), which includes the provision "Librarians must protect each user's right to privacy with respect to information sought or received, and materials consulted, borrowed, or acquired." Both recognize the chilling effect such disclosure can have on the use of library materials.

The threat is not only in the form of government authorities. Private groups and individuals might wish to expose the reading or viewing habits of certain individuals to harass or embarrass them. It is perhaps a sad commentary on the state of the public's confidence in First Amendment rights to admit that people have legitimate reasons not to have their reading or viewing habits broadcast generally or known to others. Proof of this concern can be found in passage of the Video Privacy Protection Act of 1988,[4] which prohibits the disclosure of personally identifiable information concerning any patron of a videotape service provider.

In the absence of legislation providing for privacy in the use of library materials, ALA urges that each library establish an internal policy providing for such privacy. This is sound advice, but for many public institutions such a policy would run counter to the public records laws of most states, which generally state that all the records of any agency of the state or political subdivisions thereof are open to the public for inspection. Such laws inevitably have exceptions designed to protect legitimate privacy interests. Rhode Island law, for example, reads: "For purposes of this chapter the following records shall not be deemed public . . . (21). Library records which, by themselves, or when examined with other public records, would reveal the identity of the library user requesting, checking out, or using any library materials."[5] At present, forty-four states and the District of Columbia have adopted some form of legislation protecting the privacy of library users.

The point of such legislation is to assure the library patron that he or she need not avoid certain materials for fear that the use will be interpreted unfavorably by others in the general public or by government officials. Whether that would ever happen is immaterial. It is the fear of its happening that does the mischief, and this, as with all other impediments to information, ought to be eliminated wherever possible.

Privacy Concerns of Employees

Dress Codes

It is well accepted that an employer has the right to impose a certain level of dress to comport with the image the employer seeks to establish with the public. On the other hand, it is also well recognized that dress is a matter of individual expression and that within the bounds of decency, people should be able to wear whatever clothing suits them. The arguments are irreconcilable. The public does form an opinion of an enterprise based on the dress of its employees, while the employee is at least as productive wearing running shorts as wearing a suit. The courts have generally determined that where the employee is in contact with the public, the employer has a right to prescribe the appropriate dress, but where the employee does not meet the public, the individual's preference should prevail. This seems a reasonable accommodation, but there are restrictions.

In order for the employer's wishes to prevail, there must be, in fact, a relationship between requirement and image. A school system could normally expect to enforce a requirement that male teachers wear coats and ties[6] and females acceptable skirts or dresses,[7] but it would undoubtedly be excessive to require those teachers to wear tuxedos or formal gowns. The point is that the employer has the right to set a particular tone, but whether the employer can absolutely ban certain clothing in furthering that policy is questionable. Skirts and dresses are normal and accepted garb for professional women, but to ban slacks absolutely would deprive women of the option of wearing pantsuits, which can be expensive and can evoke a very professional air.[8] Common sense is, of course, the proper approach, although the matter can be difficult to reduce to writing where a formal policy is deemed necessary. Librarians in institutions other than public libraries can be expected to conform to the dress codes or habits of the parent institution. Public libraries provide a unique situation in that on the one hand, they want to look reasonably professional, but on the other, they want to be inviting to a very diverse clientele—and looking rather starched may not be the way to do that. As a legal matter, public library administrators would probably have a difficult time in upholding a strict dress code, as it would be difficult to prove that such a code enhanced the enterprise, although requirements of decency and cleanliness would undoubtedly pass muster.

One other restriction concerning dress codes is that they must not run counter to any civil or employment rights legislation. It has been noted elsewhere that it is discriminatory to require clothing that invokes or subjects the wearer to harassment. It is also discriminatory to impose a dress code that weighs more heavily on one sex. It might be discriminatory, for example, to require women to wear tailored suits where male employees need only wear sport coats. The discrimination might come in the form of requiring one sex to spend more than the other to meet the requirements, or it might be that the regulation inhibits the choice of dress of one sex, for example, a rule that allows men but not women to wear shorts.

Grooming Codes

Grooming codes have many of the characteristics of dress codes in that employers have a right to have employees project an image favorable to the enterprise, while employees have a right to present themselves as they wish either as matter of expression protected by the First Amendment or as a privacy right. The problem is somewhat heightened, however, by the fact that many grooming characteristics are, at least temporarily, permanent. An employer may wish for short hair while the employee may have a lifestyle off the job in which long hair is desired by that individual. Since such grooming regulations impinge on the individual beyond the work environment, courts will require greater scrutiny of the necessity for the requirement than would be the case for clothing, which can be changed after working hours. Having said that, however, it must be noted that courts have gone both ways on grooming policies.[9] Many of the cases on dress codes and grooming go back twenty years to a period when appearance was often seen as a political statement. Society now seems to have a much more relaxed attitude toward these matters and issues, and outside the discrimination questions, they appear to arise only infrequently.

Residency Requirements

Many communities require their employees to reside within the community limits. It is a rule that seems to fly in the face of the individual's right to live where he or she pleases, and seems to run counter to equal protection in that it denies public employees the same freedom of lifestyle as that enjoyed by private individuals. Be that as it may, the courts have upheld such regulations.[10]

The arguments for such regulations vary depending on the particular government agency in question. In the case of police and fire fighters, the argument is that they must be reasonably close at hand in case of emergency. A distance requirement would seem more appropriate in these situations, and some communities do use that requirement. An argument often put forward in the case of other municipal employees is that the nature of their jobs requires that they be attuned to the mores of the particular community, which can only be attained through membership in that community. The real reason for such regulations lies undoubtedly in an effort to maintain or increase the community's tax base.

Whether such regulations are wise, they raise some practical problems. The most obvious legal problem lies in the meaning of residency. Clearly a post-office box is not a residency, but is a casual live-in arrangement? Suppose the employee has a seemingly valid abode within the community limits, but in fact lives with a lover in the next town? Or suppose the seemingly valid abode is out of town but the employee lives with the lover within the community? In theory the answer is where the individual actually resides, but suppose he or she actually spends time in each place? Simply put, the proof is difficult to pinpoint.

Off-Duty Conduct

It is well established that an employer has the right to discipline or discharge an employee for infractions while on the job, but to what extent does that right extend to situations that are not part of the job? It is accepted as a general rule that employers have no right to impose or restrict particular lifestyles on employees outside the workplace, providing that activity does not impede the employer's work or reflect adversely on the employer or on the individual in his or her capacity as employee.

For example, an employer may not normally fire an employee who has been convicted for reckless driving. If the conviction resulted in incarceration for a few days, dismissal would only be justified if the worker's absence was critical to the employment operation at that time. If, however, the conviction was to a bus driver, the mere conviction, let alone incarceration, would be enough to support dismissal, for it goes both to the ability of the individual to carry out his or her duties, and the unfavorable reflection on the employer that the continued employment of such drivers would produce. Either reason would be sufficient to support the dismissal.

Unconventional lifestyles are often seen as a valid cause for dismissal, but a close analysis reveals that such actions are often merely the result of raw prejudice. As with other extra-employment activity, there must be an element in which the activity complained of actually affects the employer. To some degree this is dependent on prevailing attitudes in the community. In some locales, for instance, living with a person of the opposite sex (living in sin) is seen as outrageous. If the children's librarian should take up such a living arrangement she (though quite possibly not a he) might expect to be fired. If she should become pregnant, her job might be in much greater jeopardy.

In the only such case actually involving a librarian, *Hollenbaugh v. Carnegie Free Library*,[11] in which a female librarian and the married man she was living with (a janitor in the library) were fired for living together in a state of "open adultery," the court recognized that the right of privacy encompassed and protected "the personal intimacies of the home, the family, motherhood, procreation and child rearing,"[12] but chose to find that this living arrangement was not governed by those considerations despite the fact that the couple was living together as a family, and that, as the woman was pregnant, procreation, motherhood, and childrearing were clearly involved. This case was upheld on appeal without comment, but whether it is precedent-setting is doubtful. The court in this case viewed the plaintiffs as employees-at-will who, unless they could establish their firing as a violation of constitutionally protected rights, could not prevail. This is something of an anomaly, for if they were truly employees-at-will, they could be fired for any or no reason; having constitutional protections suggests they were not employees-at-will, but rather, as government employees, had certain rights in their jobs. The court summarily dismissed these claims, and stating that it would not impose its views of the morality of the couple's living arrangement, appears to have decided the case on that basis. It seems reasonable to believe that the result of this case turned on small-town prejudices.

Other courts have come down on the other side in similar situations. In *Briggs v. Northern Muskegon Police Department*[13] the court refused to uphold the dismissal of a married police officer who lived with a woman not his wife on the grounds that such action violated the officer's right to privacy. The court looked to the question of whether the living arrangement affected the officer's job performance and rejected the argument that the dismissal could be justified by general community disapproval.

Police officers figure rather prominently in these off-duty conduct cases. Many of them turn on the fact that the activity engaged in is illegal and that police officers, as enforcers of the law, ought to be held to strict standards in obeying the law. One can argue either side of that question, but librarians clearly are not law enforcement personnel and the question ought to focus purely on the effect that off-duty activities have on job performance. It might seem a valid argument that a children's librarian is a role model, and that if that librarian is "living in sin" she presents an adverse picture to her young patrons. But the question arises as to whether those children have any concept of "living in sin" and whether the librarian's role extends beyond the immediate and particular interaction between the child and librarian. Community and parental prejudice ought not be the determining factor, but the courts are divided on the issue.

Other Invasions of Privacy

Searches

Employers are generally the owners of the property in which an enterprise takes place, or if not the actual owners, the controllers of such property. As such, they generally have the right to go where they wish and inspect what they wish on those premises. There is certainly an interest on the part of the employer to protect property and to see that no activity contrary to law or the interests of the enterprise takes place on the grounds of that enterprise. However, employees have rights against unwarranted intrusion into areas considered private. The question is, what zones are legitimately private and what intrusions are unwarranted.

The Fourth Amendment guarantees the right against unreasonable searches and seizures by the government. While technically it has no effect on intrusions by private citizens,[14] there is a spillover into the privacy question and probable cause would excuse an invasion into otherwise inviolable privacy by employers in the private sector. The next question then is, what privacy does the employee have.

The Supreme Court has put forward the proposition that privacy (in terms of Fourth Amendment protection against state intrusion) is determined by one's expectation of what is private. In a case of some years ago, but still valid, the Court said "What a person knowingly exposes to the public, even in his own home or office, is not a subject of Fourth Amendment protection. But what he seeks to preserve as private, even in an area accessible to the public, may be constitutionally protected."[15] In what is, at present, the leading case concerning governmental intrusion into the workplace, *O'Connor v. Ortega*,[16] the Court discussed the right of the governmental employer to inspect areas directly concerned with the output of the enterprise versus the right of the employee to keep inviolable those areas in which there is a reasonable expectation of privacy. The Court found that the defendant had a reasonable expectation of privacy in his office but noted that such expectations required "balancing the nature and quality of the intrusion on the individual's Fourth Amendment interests against the importance of the governmental interests alleged to justify the intrusion."[17] Such thinking makes any privacy interest vulnerable to supposed vital societal interests, and privacy will be difficult to defend in the face of politically or societally potent areas such as drug use, child abuse, or sexual harassment. Very important, however, is the fact that the decision does recognize a right to privacy within the employer's domain. The case speaks in terms of Fourth Amendment rights against government intrusion, but it has application to the private sector in which persons have a right to be free from incursions into their personal zones of privacy. In both public and private sectors, then, privacy can be understood as applying to those zones in which it is reasonable for the individual to expect to be free from intrusion. That expectation is governed in large part by the employer's policy concerning privacy and searches. The owner of a diamond mine would have the right to search departing employees each day as part of an announced security program, and on the same theory, the management of a rare book collection would have the right to inspect brief cases and bags of employees going off duty. The heart of the matter is to provide notice as to where one cannot expect privacy, and of course, apply the policy consistently.

Drug Testing

The use of drugs is thought by the general public to be a problem of great concern, and any person found to have used drugs prior to any incident causing harm is assumed to have been influenced by that drug use. This attitude produces great pressure on employers to insure that their employees are not influenced by drugs. The determination requires testing, which runs into Fourth Amendment questions if the employer is a branch of the government, and privacy considerations if private.

While there is theoretically a distinction between public and private sector employers in the right by the employer to conduct random or routine drug tests, the requirements are much the same: the employee must be engaged in an occupation involving public safety. The interpretation of what is implicated in public safety can be very broad, but so far, the courts have focused on trans-portation,[18] drug enforcement,[19] and the carrying of firearms.[20] Otherwise, there is generally a requirement of probable cause or reasonable suspicion before an employer can require a test for drugs.[21]

Many states have laws severely restricting the use of drug testing. In Rhode Island, for example, testing, except for certain federally regulated occupations, is forbidden unless there is probable cause that requires both grounds to believe there is use *and* that the use impairs job performance. Further, Rhode Island requires that the test be done by the best testing procedures available, and that if the test is positive, the employee has the right to a retest. The employee also has the right to explain the results (evidently poppy seeds and certain medication can trigger a positive result). Finally, such testing can only be done if there is a rehabilitation program operating in conjunction with the testing program. The intent of the legislation is to provide aid for the drug user, not to punish the individual. Many states have similar legislation.

Medical Records

Information concerning an employee's physical or mental health can provide an employer useful guidance in assigning work, providing assistance to the individual, and providing for safety and well-being of fellow workers. Such information can also be used improperly in reaching adverse employment decisions on employees. Whether or not medical information is used with a benign purpose, the information may be an embarrassment the individual may not wish to have disseminated. There are several mechanisms available to the individual to protect against a disclosure of one's medical records.

Invasion of Privacy

As noted at the beginning of this section on privacy, one of the elements of a privacy action is the public disclosure of private facts. Because the problem of medical records usually begins with a doctor's examination, and because there is commonly understood to be a confidential relationship between the patent and the doctor, a closely related tort is a breach of a confidential relationship. These torts are recognized in many states, though not all. A typical situation arises when the employer suggests that an employee see the company doctor or one under contract to handle the company's medical matters. The employ-ee sees the doctor, is diagnosed as having some condition detrimental to the employment situation, and that information is conveyed to the employer. The employer then distributes the information to those persons presumed to need that information: supervisors, staff medical personnel, and various managers, and, necessarily, to all the clerical people who provide support for these peo-ple. The whole situation raises several legal questions.

The first question is whether the doctor has any duty of confidentiality toward the employee who was examined. In the important case of *Bratt v. International Business Machines*, the court noted "When an employer retains a physician to examine employees, generally no physician-patient relationship exists between the employee and the doctor."[22] This is perhaps the general rule, although in this case, the court found particular circumstances in which the plaintiff could establish a confidential relationship. Establishing such a relationship is, of course, necessary to prevail in a breach of confidentiality claim, but even if that claim were not alive, establishing the duty would enhance a breach of privacy claim.

The various courts are not in complete accord in dealing with breach of privacy claims. In Massachusetts, the matter is one of balancing the privacy interests of the individual against the employer's legitimate business interest in obtaining and publishing of personal information.[23] Other jurisdictions will look closely to the elements of the tort, as they understand them, and see if they have been met. Missouri, for example, has adopted the rule, put forward in *Childs v. Williams*, that the tort of public disclosure of private facts involves (1) publication or publicity, (2) absent any waiver or privilege, (3) of private matters in which the public has no legitimate concern, (4) so as to bring shame or humiliation to a person of ordinary sensibilities.[24] In a situation of the type under discussion, it is difficult even to get beyond the first requirement. The *Childs* court, following the respected *Restatement (Second) of Torts,* found that the dissemination of the information had to be to the general public or communicated in such a way that the information is likely to become public knowledge. Informing key elements of management of an employee's medical condition simply does not meet the element of the tort. The question of waiver is simply one of fact, but the third and fourth elements can be difficult to overcome should one get past the first. Presumably a situation could exist where enough of management has been informed to satisfy a court that the information has been made public, but all members of that public, being management, might have a legitimate concern in the information. Finally, a dispassionate consideration of any medical condition ought to result in a conclusion that no medical condition warrants shame or humiliation, but it must be admitted that society does impose burdens on certain conditions and the lack of logic is no defense. Still, many medical conditions would not bring on a sense of shame or humiliation in a person of ordinary sensibilities, and even though those things might seem nobody's business, they will not support the tort claim.

Promises of Confidentiality

The National Institute on Alcohol Abuse has reported that eighty percent of the Fortune 500 companies have employee assistance programs (EAPs).[25]

These programs are designed to provide a wide range of assistance to employees with problems including alcohol and drug abuse, smoking, eating disorders, and medical matters. It is generally recognized that for such programs to be successful, the client must be confident that the program is solely for his or her benefit, and that recourse to the program will not jeopardize the employee's standing with the employer. To that end it is common practice for employers to assure confidentiality of any information generated by participation in the program.

The promise of confidentiality is normally communicated to the employee in a handbook of employee benefits or some similar document. As with statements implying a contract for employment discussed in chapter 3, courts in some states will find the promise a legally binding contract. In *Woolley v. Hoffman-LaRoche*, for example, the New Jersey Supreme Court stated that "when an employer of a substantial number of employees circulates a manual that, when fairly read, provides that certain benefits are an incident of the employment . . . the courts should construe them in accordance with the reasonable expectations of the employees."[26] It is recognized there are some situations that absolutely require disclosure, such as a diagnosis that an employee has a highly communicable disease requiring all who have had contact with that person to take preventive action. The prudent employer, therefore, will not promise absolute confidentiality but, at the same time, must offer sufficient assurances to encourage employees to make the most advantageous use of services offered.

Codes of ethics for psychiatrists, psychologists, social workers and other professionals connected with EAPs may also provide for confidentiality of clients records. Employers should understand and respect these codes, but they should not assume that such codes are a sufficient shield in themselves obviating any particular measures by the employer.

Privacy Legislation

Many states have legislation that provides tort remedies where physicians disclose confidential information between themselves and their patients.[27] In addition, many states have legislation that exempts medical records of state operated medical facilities from open records laws.

AIDS

Acquired Immune Deficiency Syndrome (AIDS) is a medical condition that in recent years has probably caused more concern than any other. The concern is well placed in that there is, at present, no cure for the condition, but the situation is exacerbated by a large degree of ignorance with regard to the susceptibility to contagion the disease carries.

As an employment issue, two things must be considered: (1) medical opinion is that AIDS, or its precursor, HIV, cannot easily be transmitted in the normal course of interpersonal relations in the workplace, and (2) AIDS is considered a disability. The first condition suggests that employers need not be excessively agitated over the danger that individuals who have AIDS or test positive for HIV pose to fellow workers. One court, summarizing findings from a lower court, found the risk of transmission of the AIDS virus by employees "minuscule, trivial, extremely low, extraordinarily low, theoretical, and approaching zero."[28] The second indicates that employers must be very careful in dealing with the problem, for almost any adverse policy directed at persons with AIDS will be interpreted as discriminatory.

Most states have legislation forbidding the testing of employees or job applicants for AIDS, which, along with the restrictive prohibitions of medical testing for employment under the ADA, essentially prohibits AIDS testing.

Conclusion

Privacy contributes to the establishment of individuality and the feeling of self-worth, but it also deprives an employer of information useful in maximizing the utilization of the workforce. As with so many issues, there is a requirement to balance the interests of employers and employees. Beyond that, however, current management theory suggests that greater productivity along with greater employee satisfaction can be gained by recognizing the value of empowering employees to respond to the needs and expectations of the enterprise and its clientele. Such empowerment requires respect for the individual and, in that, lies a respect for that individual's privacy.

NOTES

1. 381 U.S. 479 (1965).

2. New York: Atheneum, 1967, 32–39.

3. "Privacy as an Aspect of Human Dignity: An Answer to Dean Prosser," *New York University Law Review* 39 (1964):971.

4. 18 U.S.C.S. 2710.

5. Rhode Island General Laws 38-2-2.

6. East Hartford Education Assn. v. Board of Education of the Town of East Hartford, 405 F.Supp. 94 (1975). The Court found the school board had a legitimate interest in establishing minimum standards, which here required male teachers to wear neckties.

7. Tardiff v. Quinn, 545 F.2d 761 (1976). The Court upheld the dismissal of a teacher for wearing miniskirts.

8. Some courts disagree on this point. See Lanigan v. Bartlett & Co., 466 F.Supp. 1388 (1979), where the court found a rule against pantsuits in executive offices was not discriminatory under Title VII and therefore the company was free to discharge the plaintiff for infraction of the rule.

9. See, for example, Ball v. Kerrvill Independent School Dist., 529 S.W.2d 792 (1975) upholding the right to wear beards; Woods v. Safeway Stores, Inc., 579 F.2d 43 (1978) found a "no-beards" policy justified by a legitimate business purpose.

10. The controlling case is McCarthy v. Philadelphia Civil Services Commission, 424 U.S. 645 (1976) where the Court found residency requirements rational and not in violation of the right to travel. The Court distinguished this from its ruling that found unconstitutional (because it restricted the right to travel) requirements of residency of a particular length of time in order to qualify for a benefit such as welfare.

11. 436 F.Supp. 1328 (1977).

12. Id. at 1333.

13. 563 F.Supp. 585 (1983), affirmed 746 F.2d 1475 (1984).

14. The question generally arises in connetion with evidence gained by private individuals in circumstances that would have violated the Fourth Amendment had the action been carried out by governmental officials. Such evidence is usually found admissable.

15. Katz v. U.S., 389 U.S. 347, at 351 (1967).

16. 480 U.S. 709 (1987).

17. Id. at 719.

18. See Skinner v. Railway Labor Executives Ass'n, 489 U.S. 602 (1989).

19. National Treasury Employees Union v. Von Raab, 487 U.S. 656 (1989).

20. Id. Von Raab dealt with regulations of the U.S. Customs Service.

21. For a recent example, see Ritchie v. Walker Mfg. Co., 963 F.2d 1119 (1992).

22. 785 F.2d 352, at 362 (1986) quoting the Massachusetts Supreme Judicial Court to whom the question had been certified.

23. See Bratt, supra.

24. 825 S.W.2d 4 at 7 (1992).

25. Stated in Ira M. Shepard, *Workplace Privacy* (Washington, DC: Bureau of National Affairs, 1989) at 311.

26. 491 A.2d 1257, at 1264 (1985).

27. See particularly the annotation "Physician's tort liability for unauthorized disclosures of confidential information about plaintiff," 48 ALR 4th 668.

28. Glover v. Eastern Nebraska Community Office of Retardation, 867 F.2d 461 (1989).

5

CENSORSHIP

The preeminent function of any library is to provide for the communication of knowledge, information, and ideas. Anything that gets in the way of this communication is anathema to librarians. Censorship is one such intrusion that librarians vigorously, and nearly unanimously, oppose, for it strikes at the heart of librarianship. The fact that librarians hold the view that libraries ought to contain a diversity of viewpoints assures that someone will find material antithetical to his or her point of view. This is natural, but some who find material objectionable feel that the proper treatment of such material is to make it unavailable. This is what librarians oppose.

Background

The dissemination of unpopular or contrary ideas has long been thought to be dangerous. While many ordinary people may be appalled by a particular thought, historically it has been the people in power who sought laws and measures designed to curtail dissident expression, for such expression was seen as inimical to their retention of power. Throughout the later Middle Ages, the Church fought numerous sects by banning and punishing heretical expression. With the rise of secular power in the sixteenth and seventeenth centuries, the major effort in censorship shifted to a concern for sedition and what English law called seditious libel.

The rise of democracies in the western world in the nineteenth and twentieth centuries has caused some peculiar shifts in the concerns of censors; but it should not be thought that the powerful no longer attempt to control expression. In the United States alone, recent decades have witnessed many examples: the Pentagon Papers case, the Frank Snepp case, the careful control of correspondents during the Gulf War, and the proscription against any information on abortion by physicians in family planning clinics receiving any federal support, among many others. The point here is to indicate that censorship as a tool of government still exists. It may be that in the interests of public policy these and other instances of censorship are justified. Still, with narrow exceptions, it is a strong current of thought in democratic cultures that the people are best served by being informed, and that informed people make the best choices.

117

Obscenity

Depictions and descriptions of sexual activity became the focus of the censor in the nineteenth and twentieth centuries. The reasons for this are not at all clear; but one can note parallel developments that may have influenced the concern over sexuality. The period saw the rise of the middle class, which, for various reasons, developed a protectionist attitude toward women; saw the Industrial Revolution, which brought urbanization with its reduction of social control by local communities and development of a proletariat; and saw an increase in literacy by the lower classes. Given these conditions, upper classes presumed that exposure to explicit sexual materials, that is, obscenity, would result in rampant antisocial behavior, particularly on the part of the lower classes. Despite the lack of satisfactory empirical underpinnings, however, both courts and legislatures throughout the western world have assumed obscenity is a harmful matter, properly the subject of control by the various governments. It will be seen that this has not changed over the past two centuries, at least in the American experience. An analysis of that experience and its British antecedents follows.

A Brief History

The crime of obscenity (obscene libel it was called in the English system) got off to a slow start in the English courts. A man named Read was indicted in 1708 for writing *Fifteen Plagues of a Maidenhead*, but the court, in very summary fashion, stated that such a book was not indictable but punishable only in the spiritual court.[1]

In 1727 another English court found otherwise, however. In the case *Rex v. Curll*, Edmund Curll was convicted of obscene libel for publishing *Venus in the Cloister, or the Nun in her Smock*.[2] The argument in the case was whether obscenity was a spiritual or a temporal matter. The Attorney General put forward the argument that publishing obscene materials is an offense at common law, as it tends to corrupt the morals of the king's subjects, and in doing so, destroys the peace of the government, "for government is no more than publik order, which is morality." The justices evidently agreed with this, for they unanimously determined that such an offense was against the government and could be tried in the temporal courts. It might be noted that this court was the first, in a long line of courts, to determine that obscenity is indictable without addressing the question of what constitutes obscenity. Moreover, this court was the first in a long line of courts that failed to indicate any test by which to determine whether the material in question is, or is not, destructive of morality, or how the material in question is to work its supposed wickedness.

Over 100 years later, an English court did fashion a test for obscene materials that became the rule in both English and American courts. The rule evolved in the case of *Regina v. Hicklin*.[3] Henry Scott had been indicted for distributing a pamphlet entitled "The Confessional Unmasked: Showing the Depravity of the Romish Priesthood, the Iniquity of the Confessional and the Questions Put to Females in Confession." Tried before Recorder Hicklin, the case was dismissed for lack of the necessary intent to sell for profit, required under the Obscene Publications Act of 1857. The work was salacious, and on appeal, Justice Cockburn found the work obscene (the profit requirement notwithstanding), and stated his now famous "Hicklin test," which read: "The test of obscenity is this, whether the tendency of the matter charged as obscenity is to deprave and corrupt those whose minds are open to such immoral influences, and into whose hands a publication of this sort may fall."

The objections to the Hicklin test are now obvious. The test is based on the assumption that "unpure" thoughts are harmful. Obscenity fosters these "unpure" thoughts and therefore is to be proscribed. After making these assumptions, Cockburn established a measure based on the susceptibility of those individuals least able to withstand sexually suggestive material. Material found to be improper for children and the weak minded, and, evidently, members of the lower classes, is banned for everyone if the publication may fall into the hands of such people. In short, *Regina v. Hicklin* made clear three things:

1. that material could be prohibited solely for sexual content
2. that a work could be banned from general circulation if it tended to deprave or corrupt only the most immature or susceptible people
3. a work could be suppressed on the basis of isolated passages

American courts invoked the Hicklin rule first in the 1879 case *United States v. Bennett*.[4] From its adoption by U.S. courts in *Bennett* until the *Ulysses* case in 1933, the Hicklin test was the standard, the model, against which obscene materials were to be measured. It was not until 1957 that the United States Supreme Court overruled, in *Butler v. Michigan*. This legislation embodied the principle that children were to be the measure of what material was permissible for use by the general public.

While the Hicklin test maintained its vitality at least to *Ulysses*, courts quite early began modifications. For example, *In Re Worthington*[5] offered two new considerations to the matter. This was a civil proceeding to determine whether expensive editions of classic literature owned by the bankrupt Worthington Book Publishing Company might be sold by the receiver. The court noted that "certain parties," presumably Anthony Comstock of the New York Society for the Suppression of Vice, felt the books in question were "Immoral literature" and ought not be sold. Under threat of court action, the receiver sought the court's permission to sell the works.

The titles involved were *Arabian Nights*, Fielding's *Tom Jones*, the works of Rabelais, Ovid's *Art of Love*, the *Decameron* of Boccaccio, the *Heptameron* of Queen Margaret of Navarre, the *Confessions* of J. J. Rousseau, *Tales from the*

Arabic, and *Aladdin*. Judge Morgan J. O'Brien held that the books were not obscene, and in so doing advanced what later came to be known as the "whole book theory." He remarked that "a seeker after the sensual and degrading parts of a narrative may find in all these works, as in those of other great authors, something to satisfy his pruriency," but, he continued, "to condemn a standard literary work, because of a few of its episodes, would compel the exclusion from circulation of a very large proportion of the works of fiction of the most famous writers of the English language." The whole book theory, that a work could not be condemned merely because isolated passages considered out of context were thought obscene, was a significant departure from the Hicklin test as it was applied by the courts. As noted above, the Hicklin decision itself had been based on the offensiveness of only a portion of the *Confessional Unmasked*, and subsequent courts habitually followed this lead. Along with the whole book theory, Judge O'Brien seemed to suggest that a work's status as a classic put it beyond the category of obscenity. "It is," he said, "very difficult to see upon what theory these world renowned classics can be regarded as specimens of that pornographic literature which it is the office of the Society for the Suppression of Vice to suppress. . . . The very artistic character, the high qualities of style . . . make a place for such books of the character in question, entirely apart from such gross and obscene writings as it is the duty of the public authorities to suppress."

A third argument Judge O'Brien relied on was that these works were not likely to fall into the hands of those who would be adversely affected by them. Following a trend of long standing, the Judge assumed that those "whose minds are open to such immoral influence" belong to the lower, poorer classes.

He stated: "There is no such evil to be feared from the sale of these rare and costly books as the imagination of many well disposed people might apprehend. They rank with the higher literature, and would not be bought nor appreciated by the class of people from whom unclean publications ought to be withheld."

Other judges also recognized the shortcomings of the test. In 1913 Judge Learned Hand, then of the Federal District Court in New York, in connection with a case concerning the novel *Hagar Revelly*, had this to say of the Hicklin test:

> I hope it is not improper for me to say that the rule as laid down, however consonant it may be with mid-Victorian morals, does not seem to me to answer to the understanding and morality of the present time, as conveyed by the words "obscene, lewd, or lascivious." I question whether in the end men will regard that as obscene which is honestly relevant to the adequate expression of innocent ideas, and whether they will not believe that truth and beauty are too precious to society at large to be mutilated in the interests of those most likely to pervert them to base uses. Indeed, it seems hardly likely that we are even today so luke-warm in our interest in letters or serious discussion as to be content to reduce our treatment of sex to the standard of a child's library in the supposed interest of a salacious few, or

that shame will for long prevent us from the adequate portrayal of some of the most serious and beautiful sides of human nature. . . . If letters must, like other kinds of conduct, be subject to the social sense of what is right, it would seem that a jury should in each case establish the standard much as they do in cases of negligence. To put thought in leash to the average conscience of the time is perhaps tolerable, but to fetter it by the necessities of the lowest and least capable seems a fatal policy.[6]

Reasonable as the statement is, it has to be noted that Judge Hand failed to invoke his own thinking in deciding the matter before him. Rather, in view of the doctrine of *stare decisis* (which requires judicial adherence to settled principles), he relied on the Hicklin test.

A number of cases prior to the 1930s evinced a social concern with obscenity, but few did more than edge the Hicklin Rule in one direction or another. The decade of the 1930s, however, seemed to signal a change in attitudes toward morality. Random House publisher Bennett Cerf felt the change and thought it time to test the acceptability of James Joyce's *Ulysses*. In 1933, a copy of the work was imported. Duly impounded by a customs agent, the Customs Bureau brought action in federal court. The case was heard before Judge John M. Woolsey without jury.

It is not without some significance to the outcome of the case that Woolsey was a man of great culture and sound education. Fifty years old, he had been schooled at Phillips Andover Academy, Yale University, and Columbia Law School and was a collector of art and rare books. He was known as the "literary jurist" and his *Ulysses*[7] decision certainly added luster to this sobriquet.

Woolsey based his opinion on several principles, all of which had been used before in judicial decisions, although never before with such eclat. He began by examining whether the intent of the author was to exploit obscenity, and he found "in 'Ulysses,' in spite of its unusual frankness, I do not detect anywhere the leer of the sensualist." He further found that the book was sincere and honest, and although containing "many words usually considered dirty, I have not found anything that I consider to be dirt for dirt's sake. Each word of the book contributes like a bit of mosaic to the detail of the picture which Joyce is seeking to construct for his readers."

While the phrase "dirt for dirt's sake" was quickly seized as another term for pornography, Woolsey's meaning turned on the concept of relevancy. Words relevant to the story could not be found to condemn the work. In particularly felicitous phrasing, Woolsey noted in an oft quoted paragraph:

The words which are criticized as dirty are old Saxon words known to almost all men and, I venture, to many women, and are such words as would be naturally and habitually used, I believe, by the types of folk whose life, physical and mental, Joyce is seeking to describe. In respect of the recurrent emergence of the theme of sex in the minds of his characters, it must always be remembered that his locale was Celtic and his season Spring.

In addition, Woolsey ratified the particularly important concept that a work must be judged "as to its effect on a person with average sex instincts—what the French call *l'homme moyen sensuel.*" This seems eminently reasonable, but only twenty years previously Learned Hand, arguing, in *Kennerly*, for such a standard, had ultimately based his decision on the Hicklin test. Woolsey's decision was upheld two to one on appeal, but the dissenting judge, Manton, argued vigorously that the proper measure for judging obscenity was the Hicklin test, which ought to have been used to judge *Ulysses*.[8] Morris Ernst, the lawyer for the defense, found the decision a major event in the history of the struggle for free expression, saying "it would be difficult to overestimate the importance of Judge Woolsey's decision." While some scholars are less enthusiastic, it is fair to accord the decision high marks. Its importance is now faded largely because works of literature are seldom subjects of obscenity cases. And while fiction is often challenged, particularly in the schools, it is on the grounds that the material is "inappropriate" and not that it is legally obscene. When books were being taken to court, however, the Woolsey decision provided an intelligent and enlightened approach to the analysis of literature as obscenity. See, for example, Judge Frederick van Pelt Bryan's opinion in the case against *Lady Chatterley's Lover*.[9]

Ulysses was a landmark, but it did not result in any reduction in the number of cases brought to trial. Quite the opposite occurred, not because of *Ulysses* but because of the increasingly frank treatment of sex in modern literature. By one measure, the number of major cases brought in both state and federal courts between 1930 and 1950 was double the number of such cases brought between 1900 and 1930. The decade of the fifties saw an increase of twenty-five percent over the previous two decades, and the sixties more than doubled the number of cases brought in the fifties. These cases show a general trend toward greater acceptance of sex in literature, but always on the grounds of literary merit, that is, that sex was integral to the material, and not "dirt for dirt's sake," and a perception that society generally had reached a somewhat more mature attitude toward the subject of sex. None was decided on First Amendment grounds of freedom of speech or press. The typical understanding of constitutional protection for obscene materials was put forward in *Chaplinsky v. New Hampshire*, wherein the court said:

> There are certain well-defined and narrowly limited classes of speech, the prevention and punishment of which have never been thought to raise any Constitutional problem. These include the lewd and obscene, the profane, the libelous, and the insulting or "fighting" words—those which by their very utterance inflict injury or tend to incite an immediate breach of the peace. It has been well observed that such utterances are no essential part of any exposition of ideas, and are of such slight social value as a step to truth that any benefit that may be derived from them is clearly outweighed by the social interest in order and morality.[10]

However, courts were beginning to realize that there were constitutional dimensions to the question of obscenity. In *Winters v. New York*, 333 U.S. 507 (1948), a case testing the validity of a New York obscenity statute that forbade the distribution of lurid depictions of crime, the Supreme Court noted that freedom of speech and press are protected from state interference by the Fourteenth Amendment, but rather than finding the materials in question protected, the Court found the statute void for vagueness. The Court wouldn't deal directly with the obscenity question until 1957. In 1949 Judge Curtis Bok of the Pennsylvania County Court of Quarter Sessions issued a particularly searching opinion in *Commonwealth of Pennsylvania v. Gordon*,[11] a case involving nine generally respected novels: James T. Farrell's Studs Lonigan trilogy and *A World I Never Made*; William Faulkner's *Sanctuary* and *Wild Palms*; *God's Little Acre* by Erskine Caldwell; Calder Willingham's *End as a Man*; and *Never Love a Stranger* by Harold Robbins. The opinion is unusual in several respects: first, because it was written by a state trial court judge, and such judges typically do not write opinions; second, it is a particularly thoughtful opinion that includes a history of obscenity opinions; and finally, because Judge Bok recognized the necessity of approaching obscenity in light of free speech as that guarantee had been interpreted by the courts. To be indictable, a work had not only to excite sexual thoughts, but must manifest "a reasonable and demonstrable cause to believe that a crime or misdemeanor has been committed or is about to be committed as the perceptible result of the publication and distribution of the writing in question: the opinion of anyone that a tendency thereto exists or that such a result is self-evident is insufficient and irrelevant. The causal connection between the book and the criminal behavior must appear beyond a reasonable doubt." While extremely interesting, this line of reasoning has not been followed by other courts.

In 1957 the Hicklin test finally arrived before the Supreme Court of the United States in the guise of a Michigan statute that made the selling of sexually oriented materials "manifestly tending to the corruption of the morals of youth" a misdemeanor even if sold to an adult. Michigan, in *Butler v. Michigan*, argued that the statute was necessary to protect the general welfare, but, said the Court, "Surely, this is to burn the house down to roast the pig." Finding the legislation not reasonably restricted to the evil it is to avert, the Court found it unconstitutional, thus ending, at long last, the use of the most vulnerable as the measure of obscenity.

While *Butler* effectively ended the Hicklin test, the case was actually decided on the basis of overbreadth. It wasn't until four months later that the Court finally faced the question of obscenity per se. In *Roth v. United States*,[12] the dispositive question was whether obscenity "is utterance within the area of protected speech and press" (at 481). Quoting the statement from *Chaplinsky v. New Hampshire* noted above, and finding that the Court had in numerous cases assumed that obscenity was not protected by the freedoms of speech and press, Justice Brennan held that obscenity is not within the area of constitutionally protected speech.

With obscenity carved out of constitutional protection, the definition of obscenity becomes critical. In *Roth*, Brennan was careful to distinguish between sex and obscenity. Obscene material was material that dealt with sex in a manner appealing to prurient interest, whereas "sex, a great and mysterious motive force in human life, has indisputably been a subject of absorbing interest to mankind through the ages; it is one of the vital problems of human interest and public concern." As a vital problem of public concern, information concerning sex is protected, as are all ideas having even the slightest redeeming social importance. Because obscenity is utterly without redeeming social importance, it is not protected by the Constitution. Further, Brennan rejected the Hicklin test as being unconstitutionally restrictive and remarked approvingly on a test developed by the lower courts: whether to the average person, applying contemporary community standards, the dominant theme of the material, taken as a whole, appeals to prurient interest.

Roth set forth a number of the elements that were elaborated in subsequent cases and culminated in a three-pronged test propounded in *A Book Named "John Cleland's Memoirs of a Woman of Pleasure" v. Attorney General of Mass.*[13] The three prongs are (1) the dominant theme of the material taken as a whole appeals to a prurient interest in sex; (2) the material is patently offensive because it affronts contemporary community standards relating to the description or representation of sexual matters; and (3) the material is utterly without redeeming social value. The decision was decided six to three; but only two justices joined Brennan. Three others concurred in the result, each for reasons of his own, and three other justices dissented, again each for reasons of his own. Thus, the case engendered seven separate approaches to the matter of obscenity and left the field in something of a state of confusion. Justice Harlan, two years later, noted that in the thirteen obscenity cases since *Roth* in which a signed opinion had been written, there had been a total of fifty-five separate opinions. Said he, "The upshot of all this divergence in viewpoint is that anyone who undertakes to examine the Court's decisions since *Roth* which have held material obscene or not obscene would find himself in utter bewilderment."[14] It was not until 1973 that the Court reached a standard with which a majority agreed.

Between *Memoirs v. Massachusetts* in 1966 and the 1973 cases discussed below, the Court decided two cases of particular interest. As noted above, *Butler v. Michigan* had removed children as the measure for determining obscenity. In response to that, states began enacting legislation providing that certain materials, not obscene for adults, could be found obscene for minors, a concept known as variable obscenity. In 1965 New York passed such legislation making a misdemeanor the exposure, for profit, of sexual materials to minors under 17.

Samuel Ginsberg and his wife operated "Sam's Stationery and Luncheonette" in Bellmore, Long Island, where, among other things, they sold magazines including some so-called "girlie" magazines. Samuel Ginsberg personally sold girlie magazines on two separate occasions to a 16-year-old boy. Ginsberg was subsequently tried and convicted in the New York courts and appeal was made to the U.S. Supreme Court. Ginsberg defended on the ground that the statute unconstitutionally infringed the First Amendment rights of minors, rather than that the magazines in question were not obscene even as to minors. Hindsight suggests Ginsberg might have done better with the latter argument, as he failed with the former. The Court found that the statute merely adjusted the definition of obscenity to social realities, by permitting the appeal of this type of material to be assessed in terms of the sexual interests of minors. In other words, it is reasonable to assume that a minor would find material, tame for an adult, appealing to his or her prurient interest in sex. The state, by virtue of its concern for the welfare of minors, has the power to make this adjustment in definition. Most, if not all, states have variable obscenity statutes and *Ginsberg* continues to be the controlling interpretation. The case does raise interesting questions on the extent to which various constitutional rights apply to minors, a matter not fully adjudicated, nor within the scope of this work; but there is a certain incongruity in denying minors the right to see the expression of sex, either in words or pictures, but upholding their right to condoms, and, although circumscribed, to abortions. Reality suggests these last are necessary, and in light of that, censorship seems not to be based in reality. It appears that society is more permissive of doing than viewing.

The other case, prior to 1973, worth noting is *Stanley v. Georgia*.[15] Stanley was suspected by Georgia authorities of bookmaking and a valid search warrant was obtained to search his home for evidence of that activity. The search turned up little evidence of bookmaking; but in searching a desk in an upstairs bedroom, the authorities found three reels of 8mm film. Using a projector found in the house, the authorities viewed the film, determined it was obscene, and arrested Stanley for possessing obscene material. Stanley was convicted and the Supreme Court of Georgia affirmed. The U.S. Supreme Court reversed on the ground that the state had no right to make mere possession of obscene material a crime. Aside from the question of the validity of the seizure of the films under the search warrant, which three justices thought ought to be the question addressed, the interesting question the case presents is the extent to which other rights would logically follow the right to private possession of obscene materials. Common sense suggests that if one has the right to possess such material, one ought to have the right to purchase same, on down to the right to sell and to create obscene material. Commentators at the time saw the case as the end of obscenity litigation; and lawyers uniformly invoked the case as a defense against virtually every obscenity charge. The Supreme Court, just as uniformly, rejected these arguments.[16]

In an attempt to understand the social consequences of sexually explicit material, President Johnson established a commission whose task was to study the matter scientifically. The Commission initiated some eighty studies and came to the conclusion that pornography caused no antisocial behavior and recommended that all legal restrictions on the use of sexually explicit materials by adults be eliminated.

Not all of society was ready to embrace such findings. Richard Nixon, who was president by the time the Commission completed its work, found the report morally bankrupt, and Congress roundly denounced the findings. If politicians reflect the attitudes of their constituencies, society was not ready to give up censoring sexual materials. However, under the influence of Supreme Court decisions, the nature of what was objectionable changed.

By the end of the 1960s, censorship, by and large, ceased to be applied to the written word. True literature was well within the pale, but so also were erotic writings pretending no literary quality. The focus of censorship shifted to visual erotica including pictures, films, and nude dancing. Censorship cases continued unabated.

In the seven years between *Memoirs v. Massachusetts* and *Miller v. California*,[17] discussed below, five members of the Supreme Court had been replaced. The liberals Earl Warren, Abe Fortas, Hugo Black, and the not so liberal Tom Clark and John Marshall Harlan had been replaced by the very liberal Thurgood Marshall and the conservatives Warren Burger, Harry Blackmun, Lewis Powell, and William Rehnquist.[18] These conservative four, plus Byron White, made up a majority that, for the first time since *Roth*, agreed on an approach to dealing with sexual materials in *Miller v. California*.

June 21, 1973, was a momentous day in terms of Supreme Court obscenity decisions. No fewer than five cases, all written by Chief Justice Burger, were handed down on that occasion. In three of the cases, defendants relied on *Stanley v. Georgia*, only to find that the Court would not allow any logical steps that might seem to follow the right to read or view what you want in your own home.[19]

Of the five cases, the one to have a lasting impact is *Miller v. California*. The case involved the mailing of an advertisement for obscene materials, which itself was deemed obscene, to unwilling recipients. In the decision, Chief Justice Burger noted that no one now on the Court espoused the three-pronged test formulated in *Memoirs*.[20] In seeking to provide a more concrete test, Burger put forward a three-pronged test of his own, the first two prongs of which closely track those of *Memoirs*. The new measure of obscenity was that works, taken as a whole, must (1) appeal to the prurient interest in sex, (2) portray sexual conduct in a patently offensive way, and (3) taken as a whole, have no serious literary, artistic, political, or scientific value. The LAPS test, as the third prong is generally called, substituted for the earlier "utterly without socially redeeming value," which Burger termed an almost insurmountable hurdle. At the time of the decision there was great consternation on the part of civil libertarians that the test would prove an insufficient barrier to suppression of works that happened to have sexual content. In the nearly twenty years that have passed since *Miller*, however, wholesale suppression has not taken place, although, to be sure, there have been numerous obscenity cases during those years.

Miller provided one other change that also caused great consternation among civil libertarians, and that was a change in the community whose standards were to be the measure of whether a work was obscene. Prior to *Miller*, the Court had enunciated, beginning with *Roth*, a doctrine that works would be judged by "community standards." Later, in *Jacobellis v. Ohio*,[21] community was defined as "national," and juries were expected somehow to know the level of tolerance that supposedly existed across the nation toward sexually explicit material in order to determine the status of material at trial. This is clearly impossible, but the "national community" standard is not irrational in light of the fact that the First Amendment should apply protection uniformly across the nation.

In *Miller*, Burger recognized the difficulty of national standards and stated that "community standards" meant "local" community standards. The meaning of the term "local" initially caused some debate, for Burger had confused the matter by stating that it was "neither realistic nor constitutionally sound to read the First Amendment as requiring that the people of Maine or Mississippi accept public depiction of conduct found tolerable in Las Vegas, or New York City."[22] The meaning finally settled on the state as being the local community.

The next question to arise in connection with community standards was whether all three prongs of the *Miller* formulation were to be determined by community standards. In *Miller*, the first two prongs, appeal to prurient interest and patent offensiveness, are discussed in terms of contemporary community standards, but the third prong is not. As these two prongs deal with tolerance to sexual depictions, community standards would seem appropriate to the question. The third prong does not deal with sex per se, but with whether the work possesses serious literary, artistic, political, or scientific value. This is not a question of community approval, but rather whether a rational person would find such value in a work accused of being obscene. This is a nice distinction and one that is philosophically sound, but whether any juror could understand the distinction is questionable, and even if the distinction could be made, would any juror think his or her community standards were anything but a reflection of rational thinking? Would any juror reach a different conclusion with regard to applying the third prong to allegedly obscene material depending on whether he or she used a community standards test or a rational person test? One can only imagine the answers to these questions, but the applicable case to the general proposition is *Pope v. Illinois*.[23] In a concurring opinion to that case, Justice Scalia found a need for a reexamination of *Miller*, but as of 1993, none has been presented and *Miller v. California* remains the guiding case in determining the legality of materials alleged to be obscene.

Child Pornography

Since the late 1970s, the exploitive use of children in the production of sexually oriented visual materials has been seen as an increasingly grave problem. The Federal Government and nearly every state have legislation dealing with the production of such material, and many states also prohibit its distribution. In almost half the states there is no need to find the material legally obscene. The question of whether governments, in order to prevent the abuse of children who are made to engage in sexual conduct, may criminalize the production, distribution, and even mere ownership of material not legally obscene if that material presents visual depictions of minors in a sexually provocatively way has already been decided: they may.[24] At the heart of most child pornography legislation is the intent to limit the market for sexual materials involving minors, which in turn would reduce the incentive to use minors in the production of this sort of material. The concern for librarians lies in the possibility that, in the zeal to protect children, various pieces of legislation or interpretations thereof are so broad that they impinge on expressive materials which are protected by the First Amendment.

Legislation on point is the federal Child Protection and Obscenity Enforcement Act of 1988.[25] The act had record keeping requirements of gargantuan dimensions for any material visually depicting sexual activity, regardless of the age of the participants. The records required include the names, ages, maiden names, nicknames, and all aliases and stage names ever used by the participants, arranged for access by the name of the work or by any of the names used by the performers. These records were to be established and maintained by every entity involved in the production process and any subsequent user of the original visual depictions. Failure under the 1988 enactment to maintain such records would result in a legal presumption that the performers were under the age of 18. Also included in the Act were civil and criminal forfeiture provisions. The American Library Association and several media associations filed suit in the Federal District Court for the District of Columbia.[26] Judge George H. Revercomb found the record keeping requirements and the presumption for failure to keep records unconstitutional as well as some of the forfeiture provisions. Both sides appealed.

In light of Judge Revercomb's decision, Congress passed the Child Protection Restoration and Penalties Enhancement Act of 1990, which contains the subtitle A Restoration of Recordkeeping Requirement. This enactment drops the presumption provisions and limits the record keeping to those who are involved in "hiring, contracting for managing, or otherwise arranging for the participation of the performers depicted."[27] This language is hardly precise, but it does seem to relieve subsequent users of the visual depictions of the onus of record keeping. The question that remained was whether the burden of record keeping when focused only on the producer (presumably Congress's intent) is reasonable or whether it still constitutes a chilling factor in the production of expressive materials. On May 26, 1992, Judge Stanley Sporkin of the Federal District Court, District of Columbia, found that the provision did offend the Constitution because the Act invades the area of constitutionally protected depictions of sexual activity of adults. The Act's "primary flaw is that it applies to all depictions of actual sexually explicit conduct regardless of the age or even the apparent age of the model."[28] Whether the decision will be appealed or Congress will try another rewrite of the Act remains to be seen at this writing.

Librarians qua librarians presumably have little to fear personally from such legislation, but in their obligations to the Library Bill of Rights and the Librarian's Code of Ethics, librarians must confront censorship wherever it arises. Librarians need to keep abreast of legislation that impinges on protected expressive materials, and certainly every librarian should know the laws of the state in which he or she works concerning child protection.

Censorship in Public Schools

Schools, by their very nature, are fertile breeding grounds for censorship controversies. It is generally agreed that one of the functions of the school is to inculcate certain values thought to be necessary for living in a democratic society. Needless to say, there is much controversy as to which values those are, but the operative word is inculcate, a method of transmitting the customs and mores of society without the implications of understanding. On the other hand, it is also generally agreed that the school is the appropriate place for youth to attain facts, to learn to think, to begin to understand the world around them, and to deal with concepts and customs alien to their immediate surroundings. These two functions provide an almost inevitable tension. Success in inculcation is not aided by evidence of myriad alternatives, while true understanding *requires* the analysis of alternatives. On the one hand, limitation of certain material seems beneficial, but on the other hand it is inimical to the development of the thinking processes. Society generally, and the schools particularly, have accommodated these divergent functions by altering emphasis in accordance with age, grade level, or level of mental development. Thus, younger students are thought to be less able to reason and therefore more amenable to inculcation. As the child grows older, greater emphasis is placed on thinking and understanding. The system works reasonably well until there is disagreement on what material is appropriate for a particular age, or in a more extreme situation, where there is disagreement as to whether certain subjects, materials, or information is appropriate for any age. At bottom is the question, who decides?

The immediate answer is, the school board. Society traditionally accords school boards broad latitude in determining the appropriate subject matter and materials to be taught in the schools. This latitude is bounded by First Amendment considerations, in which various parties assert rights protected by that Amendment. Oddly, after all the cases, it still is not clear what rights each of the possible parties, that is, students, teachers, and parents, has. The United States Supreme Court has granted that the Bill of Rights has application to minors, but has refused to extend to them the full panoply of rights enjoyed by adults.[29] The Court also has said that "students in the public schools do not 'shed their constitutional rights to freedom of speech or expression at the schoolhouse gate,'" although the First Amendment rights of those students "are not automatically coextensive with the rights of adults in other settings, and must be applied in light of the special characteristics of the school environment."[30]

Teachers generally attempt to exert their rights through the concept of academic freedom. The old case of *Meyer v. Nebraska*[31] seems to support that concept. In this case, the Court found a Nebraska statute forbidding the teaching of a foreign language to grades below the ninth to interfere arbitrarily and impermissibly with the teaching of foreign language teachers, thus violating the due process clause of the Fourteenth Amendment. But the Court has not developed a doctrine recognizing academic freedom as a special category with considerations of its own, at least not at the elementary and secondary levels of education.

The last group that might seem to have a stake in the censorship equation is parents of students. Parents' rights have been recognized and upheld in certain educational situations. For example, in *Wisconsin v. Yoder*,[32] the Supreme Court acceded to the wishes of Amish parents to remove their children from school after the eighth grade, contrary to Wisconsin's compulsory school laws. In other contexts, however, the courts have not been solicitous of parents' wishes. *Mozert v. Hawkins County Public Schools*[33] involved parents who wished to have their children exempted from reading classes on the ground that the texts used were anti-Christian, exemplifying humanism, feminism, and pacifism, and contained themes of magic and the occult. The trial court found for the parents, but the appellate court reversed saying that the reading requirement merely exposed the students to the materials but involved no coercion to adopt a particular interpretation of the materials, nor did the readings burden or inhibit the students' own religious beliefs.

The Rights of School Boards

As noted above, school boards have broad, though bounded, discretion in determining what materials can be used in the curriculum and in the school library. Legal opinions differ as to whether there is a distinction to be made between curricular materials and library materials, and whether there is a difference to be made between banning the purchase of materials and the removal of materials already purchased. Lower courts have dealt with the power to ban materials from curriculums in a number of instances,[34] with some courts finding First Amendment violations and others not. Lower courts have also dealt with the question of removing books from school libraries, with similar results,[35] but on this issue the U.S. Supreme Court has spoken in *Board of Education v. Pico.*[36]

Pico is a case with some problems. The opinion by Justice Brennan attracted only two other justices, though another two voted for the result. It attracted four dissents, two quite stinging. With the changes in the membership of the Court over the past decade, it is unlikely that had the case been heard before the present Court, the outcome would have been the same. Still, it is the last case to come out of the Supreme Court on the question of removal of books from school libraries, and is therefore the controlling case.

In *Pico*, a plurality of the Supreme Court said that a school board could not remove materials from a school library simply because the board did not like the ideas contained in those materials. Such a removal impinges on students' First Amendment right to receive information and ideas. *Pico* clearly states that school boards do not have absolute power to determine the contents of the school's library, but that they do have the power to remove books and other materials from both curricular use and the library that are "pervasively vulgar," profane, or contrary to prevailing moral standards, that is, materials that are educationally unsuitable. Of course, educational unsuitability must be the true reason for removal of materials and not merely a pretextual expression for exclusion because the board disagrees with the ideas contained in the materials. Justice Brennan does suggest, by way of dictum, that had the question been a curricular one only, that is, compulsory classroom reading rather than optional reading of library books, the school board might well have defended its claim of absolute discretion "by reliance upon their duty to inculcate community values."[37]

Justice Brennan's dictum notwithstanding, it is reasonable to conclude that school boards, and a fortiori, school officials, do not have *absolute* power to determine curricular or library materials. In *Hazelwood School District v. Kuhlmeier,*[38] a case dealing with the right of school officials to oversee and censor a school newspaper, the Court spoke in terms broad enough to apply to a wide variety of curriculum decisions. Justice White said, for the majority, "Educators do not offend the First Amendment . . . so long as their actions are reasonably related to legitimate pedagogical concerns. . . . It is only when the decision to censor a school-sponsored publication, theatrical production, or other vehicle of student expression has no valid educational purpose that the First Amendment is 'so directly and sharply implicated,' as to require judicial intervention to protect students' constitutional rights."[39] Certainly such a decision cannot be motivated by an intent "to prescribe what shall be orthodox in politics, nationalism, religion, or other matters of opinion,"[40] but careful scrutiny must be made of such decisions, that school officials are not clothing incursions into First Amendment rights in the rhetoric of legitimate educational concerns. Thus, it would be appropriate to examine the true motives of school board members or school officials to answer a First Amendment challenge.

Finally, with regard to the question of censorship in the schools, two things need to be said. One, that the materials in question are never legally obscene, and two, that while knowledge of the law may convince officials of the error of their ways, the necessity to litigate and the willingness to do so may be the only solution to a controversy. Even then the outcome is never sure. To better the chances, every school library should have in place an approved collection-development policy detailing the kinds of material to be included in the collection and the procedures involved in making the decision to add or not to add material to the collection. In addition, there ought to be in place a set of procedures to be followed when a complaint is lodged. These procedures ought to be followed regardless of the position of the complainant, but unfortunately schools quite often fail to follow their own rules. Nevertheless, courts tend to favor the party which observes the rules[41] and, at the very least, having such policies is sound administrative practice.

NOTES

1. Queen v. Read, 11 Mod. Rep. 142 (1708).

2. 2 Stra. 788 (1727).

3. L. R. 3 Q. B. 360 (1868).

4. 16 Blatch. 338 (1879).

5. 30 N.Y.S. 361 (1894).

6. United States v. Kennerly, 209 F.119, 120.

7. United States v. One Book Called "Ulysses," 5 F.Supp. 182 (1933).

8. 72 F.2d 705 (1934).

9. Grove Press, Inc. v. Christenberry, 175 F.Supp. 488 (1959).

10. 315 U.S. 568 (1942) at 571, 572.

11. 66 D. & C. 101 (1949).

12. 354 U.S. 476 (1957).

13. 383 U.S. 413 (1966).

14. Interstate Circuit, Inc. v. City of Dallas, 390 U.S. 676 (1968) at 707.

15. 394 U.S. 557 (1969).

16. Charles Rembar, in a work discussing literary trials of the 1960s, declared that the meaning of the *Fanny Hill* case (Memoirs v. Massachusetts) is that there is no longer a law of obscenity as far as writers are concerned, at 490. His title was *The End of Obscenity* (New York: Random House, 1968).

17. 413 U.S. 15 (1973).

18. There is, of course, a danger in ever characterizing a justice as conservative or liberal although one can generalize. Blackmun is particularly interesting in that he is now considered one of the liberal members of the court and the question is whether this is because he has been joined by those more conservative than he thus shifting his relative position or that he has made an intellectual journey in the past twenty-two years. A little of each I think. See David G. Savage, *Turning Right: The Making of the Rehnquist Supreme Court* (New York: Wiley, 1992), for an interesting assessment of the current court.

19. In United States v. Orito, 413 U.S. 139 (1973), the Court found that the privacy of the home does not extend to commercial aircraft. In United States v. 12 200-ft. Reel Film, 413 U.S. 123 (1973), the Court would not extend the *Stanley* rationale to allow the importation of obscene material for purely private uses and, in Paris Adult Theatre I v. Slaton, 413 U.S. 49 (1973), the Court would not extend the concept of privacy in the home to allow consenting adults to view obscene materials in a theatre.

20. Even Brennan, the author of *Memoirs*, had abandoned the formulation as unworkable. See his dissent in *Paris Adult Theatre I*.

21. 378 U.S. 184 (1964).

22. 413 U.S. 15, at 32.

23. 481 U.S. 497 (1987).

24. See New York v. Ferber, 458 U.S. 747 (1982), which was the Court's initial finding that the protection of children outweighed any First Amendment considerations that might attach in legislation criminalizing nonobscene material. Osborne v. Ohio, 495 U.S. 103 (1990), in upholding a law criminalizing posses-

sion of sexual visual material involving minors, gives a full analysis of the various attacks on such legislation.

25. 18 U.S.C. 2251 *et seq*.

26. ALA v. Thornburgh, 713 F.Supp. 469 (1989).

27. 18 U.S.C.S. 2257(h)(3).

28. American Library Association v. Barr, 794 F.Supp. 412, at 417 (1992).

29. In re Gault, 387 U.S. 1 (1967).

30. Hazelwood School District v. Kuhlmeier, 484 U.S. 260 (1988) quoting first from Tinker v. Des Moines Independent Community School Dist., 393 U.S. 503, at 506 (1969) and then quoting Bethel School District No. 403 v. Fraser, 478 U.S. 675, at 682 (1986).

31. 262 U.S. 390 (1923).

32. 406 U.S. 205 (1972).

33. 827 F.2d 1058 (1987).

34. For cases finding a violation of First Amendment rights see Parducci v. Rutland, 316 F.Supp. 352 (1970), Harris v. Mechanicsville Cent. School District, 382 NYS2d 251 (1976), Pratt v. Independent School District, 670 F.2d 771 (1982). For cases not finding a violation of First Amendment rights see Minarcini v. Strongville City School District, 541 F.2d 577 (1976), Cary v. Board of Education, 598 F.2d 535 (1979), Zykan v. Warsaw Community School Corp., 631 F.2d 1300 (1980).

35. For cases finding a violation of the First Amendment see Minarcini v. Strongsville City School District, 541 F.2d 577 (1976), Right to Read Defense Committee v. School Committee of Chelsea, 454 F.Supp. 703 (1978), Salvail v. Nashua Board of Education, 469 F.Supp. 1269 (1979), Sheck v. Baileyville School Committee, 530 F.Supp. 679 (1982). For cases finding no violation of the First Amendment see Presidents Council, Dist. 25 v. Community School Board, 457 F.2d 289 (1972), Bicknell v. Vergennes Union High School Board of Directors, 638 F.2d 438 (1980).

36. 457 U.S. 853 (1982).

37. Id. at 869.

38. 484 U.S. 260 (1988).

39. Id. at 273 quoting Epperson v. Arkansas, 393 U.S. 97, at 104 (1968).

40. West Virginia State Board of Education v. Barnette, 319 U.S. 624, at 642 (1943), a truly fine decision that, amid the patriotism engendered by W.W. II, declared the government could not require students to salute the flag. The full quote is, "If there is any fixed star in our constitutional constellation, it is that

no official, high or petty, can prescribe what shall be orthodox in politics, nationalism, religion, or other matters of opinion or force citizens to confess by word or act their faith therein." Justice Robert Jackson for the Court.

41. See, for instance, The Right to Read Defense Committee of Chelsea v. School Committee of the City of Chelsea, 454 F.Supp. 703 (1978).

6

COPYRIGHT

Copyright is a matter of concern for all types of libraries for two main reasons. First, much of the material used by libraries is copyrighted and the potential for infringement is great; second, libraries have a vested interest in the promotion of science and the useful arts, which the copyright law is designed to encourage. A disregard for copyright endangers the incentives that encourage the production of intellectual property, and in the long run, reduces the availability of the very materials libraries wish to acquire. In addition, there is the simple fact that copyright infringement is breaking the law. The major problem is the determination of what, in fact, constitutes infringement.[1]

A Brief History

The copyright law in the English-speaking world began in England with the Statute of Anne passed in 1710, although other forms of protection for literary property had existed for some two centuries. That statute provided protection for authors for a limited period of years, a concept of property rights that was bitterly fought in the English courts, until finally upheld by the House of Lords in the case of *Donaldson v. Beckett*.[2] The question was whether an author had a common law right to his or her literary property, and if so, whether the Statute of Anne abrogated that right or merely provided a specific means of protection for a specific period of time, but otherwise left the common law right intact. By a vote of six to five it was determined that the statute did abrogate the common law right, and that an author's only protection for his or her literary property lay under the terms and conditions of the statute. In the United States, every state except Delaware individually enacted copyright legislation during the 1780s. While useful, this required an author to register in twelve different states in order to be protected. The Framers of the Constitution, obviously recognizing the advantages to a unified approach to the matter, included a specific section empowering the Congress to enact a national copyright law: "The Congress shall have the power . . . To promote the progress of science and useful arts, by securing for limited times to authors and inventors the exclusive right to their respective writings and discoveries. . . ."[3]

In 1790 Congress enacted the first copyright law, which protected books, maps, and charts. In succeeding years other categories were recognized and added to the list of protected works: musical compositions (1831), photographs (1865), and paintings and sculptures (1870). Paralleling the English experience, the question arose in the American courts whether the copyright law abrogated or merely provided the means for enforcement of a common law right held by the author. In the case of *Wheaton v. Peters*,[4] the Supreme Court of the United States found that no common law right existed and that any right an author had was created by the copyright law of 1790 for the limited time stated therein. The last major revision to the copyright law was enacted in 1976 and became effective January 1, 1978.

American interest in international copyright protection was slow to develop, possibly because, during the first half of the nineteenth century, American authors were unlikely to be pirated, whereas it was quite profitable in the United States to pirate foreign, and particularly British, authors. Interest in international protection among European nations culminated in the Berne Convention of 1886, but the United States did not become a signatory to this until 1988, as U.S. copyright law was not in line with the Berne approach. The major differences were the length of protection afforded and the formalities under which copyright vested.

The United States did afford copyright protection to foreign authors through the International Copyright Act of 1891, which in effect allowed foreign authors the same rights as American authors. It required, however, the same formalities of entry of title, notice of copyright in the work, deposit, and perhaps most onerous for a foreign author, American manufacture.

In 1954, the United States joined the Universal Copyright Convention, a multilateral scheme in which each signatory accords its own copyright protection to the works by a national of a member nation or to works first published within the borders of a member nation. As long as the work bore a prescribed notice, other domestic formalities were excused.

What Is Copyright?

Copyright is the legal protection granted by statute to the author or originator of literary or artistic productions, for certain periods of time, whereby that author or originator has the exclusive rights to do or authorize any of the following:

1. to copy the copyrighted work
2. to prepare derivative works based upon the copyrighted work
3. to distribute copies of the copyrighted work to the public by sale or other transfer of ownership, or by rental, lease or lending

4. to perform the copyrighted work publicly

5. to display the copyrighted work publicly

What Can Be Copyrighted?

Copyright protection applies to original works of authorship fixed in any tangible medium of expression, now known or later developed, from which they can be perceived, reproduced, or otherwise communicated, either directly or with the aid of a machine or device. Works of authorship include the following categories:

1. literary works

2. musical works, including any accompanying words

3. dramatic works, including any accompanying music

4. pantomimes and choreographic works

5. pictorial, graphic, and sculptural works

6. motion pictures and other audiovisual works

7. sound recordings

8. architectural works

In addition to the categories given above, there are two other categories granted copyright protection.

Compilations. A compilation is a work formed by the collecting and assembling of preexisting materials or data that are arranged in such a way that the resulting work as a whole constitutes an original work of authorship. For example, an anthology of poems arranged to show the unfolding of a particular style would be copyrightable, even though the poems themselves are in the public domain. It should be noted, however, that the copyright status of the works compiled does not change. Copyright only extends to the specific arrangement of those works.

Derivative works. A derivative work is a work based on one or more preexisting works in which the original work is recast into another form. Included in this category are translations, musical arrangements, dramatizations, fictionalizations, abridgments, condensations, or any other form in which a work may be recast, transformed, or adapted. As noted above, the owner of the copyright of the original work, if such copyright exists, has the exclusive right to make derivative works from the original, a right, of course, that may be passed to another in all the ways property can be transferred to another. If the original work is not under copyright, anyone may make a derivative work from it and copyright will protect that work to the extent of the author's contribution to it, as distinguished from the preexisting material employed in the work, and does not imply any exclusive right in the preexisting material. The copyright in such a work is independent of, and does not effect or enlarge the scope, duration, ownership, or subsistence of, any copyright protection in the preexisting material.

Materials Not Copyrightable

Blank Forms

Blank forms such as order forms, accounting sheets, report forms, and the like are not copyrightable presumably because they lack the requisite degree of original authorship.

United States Government Works

As a general rule, U.S. government documents are specifically exempted from copyright protection by section 105 of the act. This does not apply to state and local government publications, which may be copyrighted if those entities so choose. Nor does it apply to works created by government employees outside the scope of their employment. Generally, materials created through government support, such as grants and contracts, are not considered works of the United States government and thus are copyrightable by the author of the material. However, the United States Government is not precluded from receiving and holding copyrights transferred to it.

Machines and Useful Objects

Machines and useful objects do not fall within the subject matter that may be copyrighted. The protection of items so defined usually comes through patent or trade secret law. However, machines and useful objects may be embodied in an artistic design, which may itself be copyrighted. The determinant is whether or not the artistic creation is separable from the useful object or machine. The classic case is *Mazur v. Stein*,[5] in which a lamp, clearly a useful object, was supported by a statue, an artistic work. The court found that the statue could exist apart from the lamp and therefore was copyrightable.

Ideas, Systems, and Principles

Copyright protection does not extend to any idea, procedure, process, system, method of operation, concept, principle, or discovery, regardless of the form in which it is described, explained, illustrated, or embodied in such work. In short, copyright protects the form of the expression but not the underlying strata of fact or process.

Acquiring a Copyright

Copyright attaches when an author "fixes" his original work. Registration, copyright notices, and any other formalities, although useful in other contexts, are not necessary.

Original Authorship Requirement

Assuming that the material under question falls within the class of material that can be copyrighted, the first requirement is that the work be an *original work of the author or authors*. "Original work" means simply that the work not be a copy, although trivial changes such as a variation in typefaces will not be sufficient to qualify a work as "original." On the other hand, a work that is nearly identical to another would be copyrightable if it were truly created independently of the other.

"Original authorship" seems to carry with it an implication of creativity or artistry, and in fact, there is a requirement for some small degree of intellectual effort to be present. The Supreme Court has deemed that "sweat-of-the-brow" is insufficient in itself.[6] However, the work need not be clever, ingenious, artistic, or literary. Indeed, it can be useless in the eyes of all who behold it, but just so long as it evinces a touch of intellectual effort and is the original work of the author it is copyrightable.

The Fixation Requirement

The second requirement requisite to the vesting of copyright is that the work be "fixed" in some permanent, tangible medium from which a copy can be made. That medium may be now known or developed in the future, and may be perceived, reproduced, or otherwise communicated, either directly or with the aid of a machine or device.

Duration of a Copyright

Copyright endures for a specific number of years depending on the category of the work's creation and when it came into being. Once a work falls out of copyright it enters the public domain and can be copied with impunity as far as the copyright law is concerned.

Works created on or after January 1, 1978. With the exception of anonymous and pseudonymous works and works made for hire, copyright endures for a period that includes the life of the author plus fifty years. In the case of joint works, the period is measured by the life of the last surviving author plus fifty years.

The Copyright Office maintains records including the death dates of authors. There is a presumption that after seventy-five years from publication or 100 years from creation, the author has been dead for fifty years. A certificate from the Copyright Office stating that there is no record to the contrary is a complete defense to infringement.

Anonymous and pseudonymous works and works made for hire after January 1, 1978. Such works are protected for a period of seventy-five years from first publication or 100 years from creation, whichever expires first. Should the name of the anonymous or pseudonymous author become known before the end of such term, the term of copyright will be the life of the author plus fifty years.

Work for hire is work done by an employee as part of his or her employment or by an independent contractor hired specifically to create the particular work. The copyright of such work is owned by the employer.

Works created prior to January 1, 1978, but not published or copyrighted by that date. Such works are protected for the life of the author plus fifty years, or if anonymous, pseudonymous or works for hire, the 75/100-year term. However, in no case will the copyright expire before December 31, 2002, and if the work should be published before that date, the term of copyright will not expire prior to December 31, 2027.

Existing copyrights as of January 1, 1978. Under the former copyright law, protection was for a twenty-eight-year period renewable in that twenty-eighth year for another twenty-eight years. If, on January 1, 1978, a work was in its first twenty-eight-year term, that term continues on and is renewable in the twenty-eighth year for a term of forty-seven more years. Any copyright that was in its renewal term or registered for renewal at any time between December 31, 1976, and December 31, 1977, was extended to endure for a term of seventy-five years from the date copyright was initially secured.

Miscellaneous Considerations

There are several elements of the copyright law that, while not likely to cause concern for the librarian, are of passing interest and will be addressed here. These involve the matters of notice, deposit, registration, and moral rights. Prior to the adoption of the Berne Convention Implimention Act of 1988 (BCIA) (which took affect March 1, 1989), the law required that any published work carry notice of copyright. With the adoption of the Berne Convention, which eschews all formalities for the vesting of copyright, that notice is no longer required, although it is optional. The Act provides that notice has evidentiary weight in an action where the defense is innocent infringement; and so it would seem silly not to include the notice even though it is not required. On the other hand, librarians should be alert to the fact that the lack of a copyright notice in a work published after March 1, 1989, does not mean the work is not under copyright.

Registration of a work with the Copyright Office is not a requirement for obtaining copyright, but registration is required before one can bring suit for protection of copyright. Viewing this contrary in spirit to the Berne Convention, the BCIA maintained the registration requirement for American works, but allowed foreign works the right to sue even if not registered.

Deposit, like registration, is not a precondition for copyright. However, the law requires the deposit of two copies of published copyrighted materials with the Library of Congress within three months of the first publication, the failure of which does not effect copyright but can result in fines.

Moral Rights

The Berne Convention provided authors with certain moral rights in their works that continue independent of copyright ownership.

> Independently of the author's economic rights, and even after the transfer of said rights, the authors shall have the right to claim authorship of the work and to object to any distortion, mutilation or other modification, or other derogatory action in relation to the said work which shall be prejudicial to his honor or reputation.

American copyright law had never recognized such moral rights, and debate on the Berne Convention Implementation Act covered but dismissed any inclusion of moral rights, a fact that the BCIA does not mention.

However, an amendment (effective June 1, 1991) to the Copyright Act does provide authors of works of visual art with the right to claim or deny authorship in a particular work, and with the right to prevent distortion or mutilation that would be prejudicial to his or her honor or reputation and to prevent the destruction of a work "of recognized stature." (Section 106A). These rights last the lifetime of the author, or the last author in a joint effort, and may be waived by the author(s) but may not be transferred.

Under ordinary circumstances, the rights mentioned above would not involve librarians directly, but the same amendments included provisions (at section 113(d)) that deal with art that is incorporated in a building. These could affect librarians. In brief, if a work of visual art is incorporated in a building in such a way that its removal requires destruction or mutilation of the work, the artist and building owner should enter into an agreement nullifying the protection provided by section 106A(a)(3). Artists, of course, may not wish to grant rights to destroy their work, but without such a grant, building owners appear to be stuck in perpetuity with the art unless they can prove the work is not "of recognized stature." Works incorporated in buildings prior to the effective date of the amendment, that is, June 1, 1991, are not protected by the Act.

If a building owner wishes to remove works of visual art that can be removed without destruction, distortion, or mutilation, the author of those works retains the rights granted under section 106A, unless after a diligent, good faith effort, the author of the work cannot be found, or if found, the author fails to take appropriate action within ninety days of notification of the building owner's intention to remove the work. If the work is removed by the author, title of that copy of the work is deemed to be in the author. Presumably, if the building owner handles the removal of the work, the title is his.

Clearly, it behooves librarians and all building owners who contemplate renovations or new buildings in which visual art will be incorporated to pay close attention to section 113(d) of the Copyright Act.

The Erosion of Exclusive Rights

As noted above, section 106 of the Copyright Act gives the owner of copyright exclusive rights in the copyrighted work. Sections 107 through 119 erode those exclusive rights partly in recognition of the development of copyright law, for example, the fair use doctrine, and partly in recognition of the need to allow for specific needs, such as reproduction by libraries and archives. The discussion that follows will touch on only those areas which are most apt to affect librarians.

The Fair Use Doctrine

The fair use doctrine in the United States can be traced back to the 1841 copyright case of *Folsom v. Marsh*,[7] wherein Supreme Court Justice Joseph Story said, "We often, in deciding cases of this sort, look to the nature and objectives of the selection made, the quantity and quality of the material used, and the degree in which the use may prejudice the sale or diminish the profits or supersede the objects of the original work."

The purpose of the fair use doctrine is to allow a reasonable amount of copying, which, under a strict reading of the copyright laws enacted over the years, wasn't possible. In section 107 of the present law, the doctrine has been codified and includes, to a large extent, Justice Story's notions of fair use, although the term itself was not used until the 1860s. Section 107 specifically allows copying for purposes such as criticism, comment, news reporting, teaching (including multiple copies for classroom use), scholarship, or research. In determining whether the use made of a work in any particular case is a fair use, the factors to be considered include:

1. the purpose and character of the use, including whether such use is of a commercial nature or is for nonprofit educational purposes

2. the nature of the copyrighted work

3. the amount and substantiality of the portion used in relation to the copyrighted work as a whole

4. the effect of the use upon the potential market for or value of the copyrighted work

Several recent cases involving the fair use of unpublished materials were decided against the proposition that the use was fair. The courts took the view that unpublished material deserved greater protection than published material. The key case was *Harper & Row v. Nation* in which the Supreme Court said "the scope of fair use is narrower with respect to unpublished works."[8] In subsequent cases the lower courts followed, as they must, this interpretation.[9] As letters, diaries, notes, and all sorts of other unpublished materials are the basis for much research, scholars raised the alarm that such an interpretation of fair use with regard to unpublished materials would be a serious obstacle to research. Congress responded by adding to the four factors listed above, the following: "The fact that a work is unpublished shall not itself bar a finding of fair use if such finding is made upon consideration of all the above factors."[10]

The courts have indicated that these factors are illustrative and not exhaustive,[11] but an analysis of the cases suggests that factor four carries the greatest weight. The U.S. Supreme Court has called it "undoubtedly the single most important element in fair use."[12] Other factors the courts have used in evaluating fair use are whether the material was published or unpublished, and the means by which the copied material was obtained. Copying unpublished material is less likely to be found fair use, as is the copying of material that was stolen or obtained fraudulently. One should note that there are economic implications even if a copyrighted work is unavailable for purchase, as interest in purchasing might induce a publisher to bring out another edition or printing.

At the time of passage of the copyright law, Congress considered including specific exemptions for nonprofit educational institutions, but concluded that such exemptions were unjustified. However, the Ad Hoc Committee of Educational Institutions and Organizations on Copyright Law Revision developed a set of guidelines for classroom copying of books and periodicals in not-for-profit educational institutions. These guidelines are not part of the copyright legislation, but they were included in the Congressional Committee Report,[13] and it is widely assumed that any court confronted with a classroom copying case would rely heavily on the guidelines. The parties making up the Ad Hoc Committee were in agreement at the time that the guidelines stated the minimum and not the maximum standards of educational fair use under section 107. It appears that no case has been reported that relied on the guidelines, so their legal effect remains untested; but it does appear that educational institutions have largely followed this rather restrictive interpretation of section 107.

Guidelines for Classroom Copying of Books and Periodicals

I. Single Copying for Teachers

A single copy may be made of any of the following by or for a teacher at his or her individual request for his or her scholarly research or use in teaching or preparation to teach a class:

- A. a chapter from a book
- B. an article from a periodical or newspaper
- C. a short story, short essay or short poem, whether or not from a collective work
- D. a chart, graph, diagram, drawing, cartoon or picture from a book, periodical, or newspaper

II. Multiple Copies for Classroom Use

Multiple copies (not to exceed in any event more than one copy per pupil in a course) may be made by or for the teacher giving the course for classroom use or discussion, *provided that*:

- A. the copying meets the tests of brevity and spontaneity as defined below
- B. meets the cumulative effect test as defined below
- C. each copy includes a notice of copyright

Brevity

1. Poetry: (a) a complete poem if less than 250 words and if printed on not more than two pages, or (b) from a longer poem, an excerpt of not more than 250 words.

2. Prose: (a) either a complete article, story, or essay of less than 2,500 words, or (b) an excerpt from any prose work of not more than 1,000 words or ten percent of the work, whichever is less, but in any event a minimum of 500 words.

   [Each of the numerical limits stated in "1" and "2" above may be expanded to permit the completion of an unfinished line of a poem or of an unfinished prose paragraph.]

3. Illustration: one chart, graph, diagram, drawing cartoon, or picture per book or per periodical issue.

4. "Special" works: certain works in poetry, prose, or in "poetic prose," which often combine language with illustrations, and which are intend-

ed sometimes for children and at other times for a more general audience and fall short of 2,500 words in their entirety. Paragraph "2" above notwithstanding, such "special works" may not be reproduced in their entirety; however, an excerpt comprising not more than two of the published pages of such special work and containing not more than ten percent of the words found in the text thereof may be reproduced.

Spontaneity

1. The copying is at the instance and inspiration of the individual teacher, and
2. the inspiration and decision to use the work and the moment of its use for maximum teaching effectiveness are so close in time that it would be unreasonable to expect a timely reply to a request for permission.

Cumulative Effect

1. The copying of the material is for only one course in the school in which the copies are made.
2. Not more than one short poem, article, story, essay, or two excerpts may be copied from the same author, nor more than three from the same collective work or periodical volume during one class term.
3. There shall not be more than nine instances of such multiple copying for one course during one class term.

   [The limitations stated in "2" and "3" above shall not apply to current news periodicals and newspapers and current news sections of other periodicals.]

III. Prohibitions as to I and II Above

Notwithstanding any of the above, the following shall be prohibited:

Copying shall not be used to create or replace or substitute for anthologies, compilations, or collective works. Such replacement or substitution may occur whether copies of various works or excerpts therefrom are accumulated or are reproduced and used separately.

There shall be no copying of or from works intended to be "consumable" in the course of study or teaching. These include workbooks, exercises, standardized tests, and test booklets and answer sheets and like consumable material.

Copying shall not:

1. substitute for the purchase of books, publisher's reprints, or periodicals
2. be directed by higher authority
3. be repeated with respect to the same item by the same teacher from term to term

No charge shall be made to the student beyond the actual cost of the photocopying.

Guidelines for Educational Uses of Music

The Ad Hoc Committee on Copyright Revision and representatives of the music publishing industry and music educators' associations developed a set of guidelines for educational uses of music, which were issued the day following those guidelines for books and periodicals.[14]

Permissible Uses

A. Emergency copying to replace purchased copies which for any reason are not available for an imminent performance, provided purchased replacement copies shall be substituted in due course.

B. For academic purposes other than performance, single or multiple copies of excerpts of works may be made, provided that the excerpts do not comprise a part of the whole which would constitute a performable unit such as a section, movement or aria, but in no case more than ten percent of the whole work. The number of copies shall not exceed one copy per pupil.

C. Printed copies which have been purchased may be edited or simplified, provided that the fundamental character of the work is not distorted or the lyrics, if any, altered or lyrics added if none exist.

D. A single copy of recordings of performance by students may be made for evaluation or rehearsal purposes and may be retained by the educational institution or individual teacher.

E. A single copy of a sound recording (such as a tape, disc or cassette) of copyrighted music may be made from sound recordings owned by an educational institution or an individual teacher for the purposes of constructing aural exercises or examinations, and may be retained by the educational institution or the teacher.

Prohibitions

A. Copying to create or replace or substitute for anthologies, compilations or collective works.

B. Copying of or from works intended to be "consumable" in the course of study or of teaching, such as workbooks, exercises, standardized tests and answer sheets and like material.

C. Copying for the purposes of performance, except as in I.A above.

D. Copying for the purpose of substituting for the purchase of music, except as in I. A and B above.

E. Copying without inclusion of the copyright notice which appears on the printed copy.

Note that both the guidelines for classroom copying of books and periodicals and copying of music for educational uses of music require the inclusion of the copyright notice. With the Berne Convention Implementation Act of 1988, the requirement of copyright notice was lifted for purposes of obtaining copyright. That being the case, it seems reasonable to believe that such notice as required by the guidelines is no longer operative. On the other hand, it does no harm to include the notice and it may be a service to the user to readily ascertain that the material is copyrighted.

Copying for Reserve Use

A matter of some concern to academic libraries and occasionally to other types of libraries is the copying of materials to be put on reserve for student use. Neither the act itself nor the guidelines address the question. It appears that most academic libraries assume that such copying falls under fair use. The American Library Association in 1982 issued its *Model Policy Concerning College and University Photocopying for Classroom, Research and Library Reserve Use*, which, as the title indicates, covers copying for reserve use. The guidelines that follow are taken from the model policy.

If the request calls for only one copy to be placed on reserve, the library may photocopy an entire article, an entire chapter from a book, or an entire poem. Requests for multiple copies on reserve should meet the following guidelines:

1. the amount of material should be reasonable in relation to the total amount of material assigned for one term of a course taking into account the nature of the course, its subject matter, and level

2. the number of copies should be reasonable in light of the number of students enrolled, the difficulty and timing of assignments, and the number of other courses that may assign the same material

3. the material should contain a notice of copyright

4. the effect of photocopying the material should not be detrimental to the market for the work. In general, the library should own at least one copy of the work

The ALA guidelines go on to suggest that a reasonable number of copies will, in most cases, be less than six, and that spontaneity as defined by the guidelines on classroom copying of books and periodicals would justify copying for reserve use. These guidelines are reasonably consistent with the guidelines for classroom copying, and in following them, any library should feel sure its actions fall within the fair use exception of the copyright law. It must be noted, however, that these guidelines do not carry the imprimatur of a Congressional committee enjoyed by the other guidelines, and thus may carry less weight.

Library Copying

Section 108 of the copyright law allows libraries and archives to make a single copy under certain circumstances if the library or archives conforms to prescribed requirements: the collections of the library or archives must be open to the public or to researchers outside the particular institution, must not make the copy for any direct or indirect commercial advantage, and the copy must bear the copyright notice. If these conditions are complied with the library or archives may make a copy in the following situations:

1. A facsimile copy may be made of an unpublished work for purposes of preservation and security, or for deposit for research use in another library or archives providing that institution is open to the public or to outside researchers. It is unclear why Congress determined the copy should be in facsimile form, but a literal reading suggests that a copy in machine-readable form is not permissible. However, copies in microform or made by copy machine (which are presumed permissible) are not facsimiles in the true sense of the word either, and a reasonable interpretation would be that Congress wanted to insure the integrity of the intellectual content of the work rather than its physical form, and thus it would be permissible to convert the work to machine-readable form providing the text was unaltered. In the absence of any case interpreting the matter, this author believes that copying in machine-readable form conforms with the spirit and intent of this section.

2. A library or archive may make a facsimile copy of a published work solely for replacement purposes if the library or archives has, after a reasonable effort, determined that an unused replacement cannot be obtained at a fair price. A reasonable effort would include all the usual steps the library or archives takes to obtain new materials. The fact that the replacement is to be unused largely rules out the antiquarian book trade in satisfying the conditions of this section. [Facsimile has been discussed in 1. above.]

3. A copy may be made at the request of a user of one article or contribution to a compiled work or a small part of any other copyrighted work, and if it has been determined on the basis of a reasonable search that a copy of the copyrighted work cannot be obtained at a fair price, the library or archives can copy the whole work or a substantial part thereof, provided: (a) that the copy

becomes the property of the user and that the library is unaware of any use other than private study, scholarship or research, and (b) the institution displays prominently and includes on its order forms a warning against copyright infringement.

The Register of Copyrights has prescribed the following as the necessary warning:

NOTICE: WARNING CONCERNING COPYRIGHT RESTRICTIONS
The Copyright law of the United States (Title 17, United States Code) governs the making of photocopies or other reproductions of copyrighted material.

Under certain conditions specified in the law, libraries and archives are authorized to furnish a photocopy or other reproduction. One of these specified conditions is that the photocopy or reproduction is not to be "used for any purpose other than private study, scholarship, or research." If a user makes a request for, or later uses, a photocopy or reproduction for purposes in excess of "fair use," that user may be liable for copyright infringement.

This institution reserves the right to refuse to accept a copying order if, in its judgment, fulfillment of the order would involve violation of copyright law.[15]

4. Subsection G (2) of section 108 forbids systematic photocopying but specifically authorizes copying for interlibrary lending, provided that such arrangements "do not have, as their purpose or effect, that the library or archives receiving such copies . . . does so in such aggregate quantities as to substitute for a subscription to or purchase of such work." This wording prompted much consternation and produced yet another set of guidelines, this time devised by the National Commission on New Technological Uses of Copyrighted Works (CONTU). In summary, the guidelines provide:

1. That any requesting entity may receive in any calendar year, up to five articles published within five years from the date of the request from any given periodical. The guidelines do not cover periodical material over five years old, and the assumption must be that copying of older articles has little or no economic impact, and thus more extensive, though surely not limitless, copying would be permissible under the fair use exemption.

2. Concerning material other than periodicals, a requesting entity may obtain from another institution no more than five copies of or from any given copyrighted work, including a collective work, within any calendar year. Unlike the guideline for periodicals, this guideline applies for the duration of copyright, not just the past five years.

3. If the requesting entity has on order or owns material which it wishes copied but does not have that item available to copy, it may request a copy from another institution without that copy counting as one of the five permitted copies.

4. No request for a copy of any material to which these guidelines apply may be fulfilled by the supplying entity unless the request is accompanied by an assurance that the request is in accordance with these guidelines.

5. The requesting institution must keep records of all requests for copies and records of fulfillment of those requests for three calendar years following the year in which the request was made.

As with all the other provisions of section 108, these guidelines have not been tested in court, but it must be assumed that they would carry substantial weight should a court action occur. In any event, one would have to admit that section 108 and the CONTU guidelines are really quite generous to libraries and archives, and provide for fairly substantial amounts of copying. It must always be remembered that permissions can be requested where copying activity is beyond that permitted by the Act. There must be an affirmative answer to the request prior to such copying, of course. A mere request is not a substitute for granted permission.

Initially, section 108 had a requirement for the Copyright Office to make a report to Congress assessing the provisions of section 108 in carrying out the intent of the copyright law. That requirement was repealed by the Copyright Amendments Act of 1992.[16]

Computer Software

The computer software industry has a particularly vexing problem in the protection of its product. Software tends to be expensive and the copying of it cheap and easy. Also, software, even if not copied, can be used by many persons either serially or simultaneously. This, of course, diminishes sales and thus profits. The software industry has and continues to attempt to control both copying and use beyond the first sale with a good deal of vigor.

Computer software and computer programs are copyrightable, and are considered to belong to the category of literary works presented in section 102 of the Copyright Act. Computer programs, defined in the act as sets of "statements or instructions to be used directly or indirectly in a computer in order to bring about a certain result" (section 101), may be copied if the copy is an essential step in utilizing the computer, or if such copy is for archival purposes, that is, a back-up copy. Archival copies must be destroyed if possession of the original computer program is no longer rightful (section 117). While the ability to copy the computer program is very important in a technical sense (the machine either makes a copy or has a copy on its hard disk in order to function), the matter is not one of which librarians need a keen awareness. Software, on the other hand, is.

The copying of software is guided by the same considerations as is the copying of other literary works. The fairness doctrine is applicable, as are the provisions of section 108. That said, however, it is probably safe to say that most copying done is an infringement. The Software Publishers Association vigorously litigates software piracy when such activity (mostly by evidently disgruntled former or present employees) is brought to its attention. Libraries are not immune to this.

In attempting to control and limit the use of software after it had been sold, the software industry ran into the "first sale" doctrine, which says, in brief, that the purchaser of a copyrighted item is entitled, without permission of the copyright owner, to sell or otherwise dispose of that item. To avoid the doctrine, the software industry adopted the policy of licensing rather than selling the product to the end user. Typically, the license to which the end user agreed was indicated on the package and the opening of the package indicated the user's agreement to the terms (known generally as shrink-wrap licensing). These licenses generally fall into one of three categories:

1. Individual licenses in which the software is licensed to a particular individual. The software may be used on a variety of machines but only by the particular individual.

2. Site licenses (sometimes machine licenses), in which the software is licensed to a particular site (or machine) where anyone may use it.

3. Concurrent uses, in which the software is licensed for network use, usually limited to a maximum number of simultaneous users.

The debate over such licensing arrangements ensued for several years, and two states, Louisiana and Illinois, enacted legislation enforcing such agreements. Legal scholars debated the applicability of the Uniform Commercial Code (UCC), which defines a sale (and the licensing scheme looks pretty much like a sale). If it is a sale and not a license, what is the significance, if any, of the shrink-wrap license? The matter has been somewhat altered with the passage of the Computer Software Rental Amendments Act of 1990, which amended section 109 of the Copyright Act.

Entitled "Limitations on exclusive rights: Effect of transfer of particular copy or phonograph," section 109 provides, with a very important exception, that no one may dispose, for the purpose of direct or indirect commercial advantage, of a copy of a phonograph or computer program (which here Congress seems to equate with computer software) by rental, lease, or lending or any other act in the nature of rental, lease or lending without the permission of the copyright owner. The Act expressly exempts nonprofit libraries and nonprofit educational institutions. "The transfer of possession of a lawfully made copy of a computer program by a nonprofit educational institution to another nonprofit educational institution or to faculty, staff, and students does not constitute rental, lease, or lending for direct or indirect commercial purposes under this subsection."

The amendment goes on to give specific permission for the lending of a computer program for nonprofit purposes by a nonprofit library, so long as the packaging containing the program carries the usual warning of copyright prescribed by the Register of Copyright. The required warning reads:

Notice:

Warning of Copyright Restrictions

The copyright law of the United States (Title 17, United States Code) governs the reproduction, distribution, adaption, public performance and public display of copyrighted material.

Under certain conditions specified in law, non-profit libraries are authorized to lend, lease, or rent copies of computer programs to patrons on a nonprofit basis and for nonprofit purposes. Any person who makes an unauthorized copy or adaptation of the computer program, or redistributes the loan copy, or publicly performs or displays the computer program, except as permitted by Title 17 of the United States Code, may be liable for copyright infringement.

This institution reserves the right to refuse to fulfill a loan request if, in its judgment, fulfillment of this request would lead to violation of the copyright law.[17]

The amendment required the Register of Copyrights to make a report to Congress within three years of enactment of the amendments to section 109, that is, by the end of 1993, after consultation with copyright owners and librarians, to determine whether this proviso had achieved its intended purpose of maintaining the integrity of the copyright system while providing nonprofit libraries the capacity to fulfill their function. On its face, this proviso seems to provide an admirable balance in protecting the interests of the copyright owners while providing needed dissemination of information to the public. Note carefully that section 109 deals with the *transfer* of possession of software. It does not provide for any copying of the software transferred. The degree to which the amended section 109 affects multiple and/or network uses is not clear. On the theory that lending is a form of sharing, one could argue that network use is merely another form of lending and thus permissible.

Videotapes

Section 110 of the Copyright Act allows performances of copyrighted material in a number of special situations, most of which are not generally applicable to libraries. Subsection (1), however, is. It provides an exemption to the exclusive rights granted in section 106 for the performance or display of a copyrighted work in the course of face-to-face teaching activities of a nonprofit educational institution. In the case of audiovisual materials, the exemption applies only if the performance, or the display of individual images, is given by means of a copy that was lawfully made. Section 110 (1) gives a wide latitude in the use of copyrighted performances in the classroom, but it does not authorize the copying of copyrighted materials for that purpose. While section 110 (1) covers any format in which a performance or display can be encompassed, it is the videotape that has caused the most consternation. It was not long before it became apparent that the VCR provided an extraordinarily easy method of copying television programs, and the various elements connected with the production of television programs were not slow to see the economic consequences of widespread copying (so-called off-air taping) and subsequent use for educational purposes. The question was whether off-air taping was an infringement, and if so, whether a compromise could be reached between the producers and users of television broadcast works. As early as March, 1979, the House Subcommittee on Courts, Civil Liberties, and Administration of Justice appointed a committee consisting of representatives of education organizations, copyright proprietors, and creative guilds and unions to address this question. This committee came up with another set of guidelines interpreting the fair use of broadcast programs taped off the air.

As developed, the guidelines only apply to the use of off-air recordings by nonprofit educational institutions of broadcast television programs. Programs carried only on cable are not covered by these guidelines. Indeed, the guidelines are quite specific in defining broadcast programs as those programs transmitted by television stations for reception by the general public without charge. However, if these guidelines meet the demands of fair use in off-air taping, it is difficult to see why they would not meet the demands of fair use in off-cable taping. An intelligent interpretation would be that cable transmission poses the same tensions as over-the-air transmissions, and that these guidelines should act as safe guidance in off-cable taping. Specific guidelines are:

1. The recorded program may be retained for forty-five consecutive days after the day of recording. Upon conclusion of that period, the tape must be erased.

2. During the forty-five-day period, the program may be shown once and repeated once for educational reinforcement in the first ten consecutive school days following the taping. The tape must be shown in a classroom or other similar place of instruction. Following the first ten consecutive school days, the tape may be played only for the purpose of evaluating it for inclusion in the curriculum. It may not be used for student exhibition or other non-evaluative purpose.

3. Off-air recordings may be made only at the request of or by individual teachers. Taping may not be made by librarians or media specialists in anticipation of future use, nor may administrators direct such taping. A program

may be recorded off-air for classroom use only once at the request of or by the same teacher, regardless of the number of times the program is broadcast.

4. A limited number of copies may be reproduced from each off-air recording to meet the needs of other teachers. Each copy is subject to the limitations governing the original copy.

5. Off-air recordings need not be used in their entirety, but they may not be altered from their original content nor may they be physically or electronically combined or merged to constitute teaching anthologies or compilations.

6. All copies must include the copyright notice on the broadcast program as recorded.

7. Educational institutions are expected to establish appropriate control procedures to maintain the integrity of the guidelines.[18]

Comment

A close adherence to these guidelines would undoubtedly absolve any librarian or teacher from a charge of infringement (although the guidelines do not prevent any copyright owner from bringing suit), but there are several requirements that are questionable at best. The limitation to one showing with one more for reinforcement makes little sense. Taken literally, it would mean an absent child could not be shown the tape upon returning to class. The requirement of a classroom setting suggests that the child who had been absent could not take the tape home for viewing either. Indeed, it is difficult to see what harm to the copyright owner would result in nonstop showing of the recorded program during the ten-day window, if one could find an educational reason to do so.

Section 110 (1) and the off-air guidelines are directed at classroom use, and do not address videotape use in a library setting. Fair use is, of course, available to libraries, and libraries can copy videotapes in the limited circumstances put forth in section 108 for other materials. Generally, the showing of videotapes to the public, off-air or otherwise, would be a public performance requiring necessary performance licenses from the copyright holder. If a library had a formal education program with a space regularly used as a classroom, the library would then fall within the scope of section 110 (1) and the off-air guidelines.

Debate exists as to whether a library patron may view a videotape in the library. The argument is that this is a public performance thus requiring permission. On the other hand, that patron can borrow the tape for viewing at home. It is illogical to find infringement in the first instance when viewing the same tape at home is permissible. Of course, the library viewing would be limited to the particular patron or at most, the patron and family. It is true that in the home the group of viewers can include a small circle of friends, and as the gauge of what can be done in the library is what is permissible in the home, it would seem that some friends might also be permitted to view the tape in the library. The ice gets increasingly thin, however, as the showing edges ever closer to a public performance; libraries would be wise to limit the circle of viewers it would allow to view a protected videotape in the library. Many tapes are labeled "For home use only," but libraries should take the position that the vendor knows the library's use of the tape and authorizes that use when making the sale. The cautious librarian can always state explicitly on the purchase order the uses to which the material will be put.

As noted above, libraries may loan videotapes for personal use, but they should not knowingly be loaned to individuals or groups for the purpose of public performances. Although the Copyright Act doesn't require it, it would be good policy and consistent with other sections of the Act to include warnings against infringement on the loaned material.

Infringement Relief

Anyone who violates the exclusive rights granted in section 106 of the Copyright Act as modified by sections 107–119 is an infringer, and the owner of the copyright is entitled to sue. The statute of limitations is three years "after the claim accrues," which means three years after the owner knew or should have known of the infringement. The remedies available are injunctive relief, damages and profits, and impounding and destruction of the infringing materials. At the court's discretion costs and reasonable attorneys' fees may be awarded the prevailing party.

Of the several remedies available, damages and profits are the most likely to be brought to bear on an infringing library. There are several categories of copyright damages.

1. Actual damages. This is the amount of money lost by the copyright owner, usually through reduced sales, because of the infringement.

2. Profits. In addition to actual damages, the copyright owner has the right to recover any profits the infringer has made, unless the profits and losses amount to the same thing. For example, if an infringer copies and sells a work in competition with that of the copyright owner, the infringer's sale is directly related to the owner's failure to sell and the owner cannot collect a double recovery. However, if the sale by the infringer resulted in a failure of the owner to sell serialization rights to the local newspaper, the profit and loss are not the same thing and the copyright owner could collect both.

3. Statutory damages. Because actual damages and profits are almost always difficult to prove, the Act provides for statutory damages as an alternative if the registration requirement of section 412 of the Act has been met.

Statutory damages range from $500 to $20,000 at the discretion of the court. If the infringer acted willfully, that is, knowingly, the court may increase the statutory damages to $500,000. On the other hand, if the infringer was unaware and had no reason to believe the actions were infringing, the court may reduce the damages to $200. Further, in any case where the infringer felt, on reasonable grounds, that his or her use was a fair use under section 107, the court must remit statutory damages if the infringer was an employee of a nonprofit educational institution, library, or archives acting within the scope of his or her employment.

The Eleventh Amendment

An issue that has whetted the interest of copyright lawyers over the past several years has been the Eleventh Amendment to the Constitution of the United States. The Amendment says that the federal courts may not be used in suits against a state, and since copyright laws are the exclusive domain of federal law and the federal courts, a state and its agencies are immune to court suit. One of the peculiarities of the Eleventh Amendment is that it is not operative when there is a specific declaration by Congress that the Amendment would not apply in a specific instance. In December 1990, Congress declared that the copyright law was not impacted by the Eleventh Amendment, and thus states are not immune to copyright infringement suits. It might be noted that the individual actually doing the copying was never protected by the Eleventh Amendment from being sued personally. An interesting moral dilemma, now moot.

Notes

1. There are many good works on copyright. Among the best are *Nimmer on Copyright,* a four-volume treatise published by Matthew Bender, updated twice a year; the *Copyright Law Reporter,* a weekly loose-leaf service published by Commerce Clearing House; and, for a practical "how to" discussion there is Stephen Fishman's *The Copyright Handbook,* published by Nolo Press in 1992.

2. 4 Burr. 2408 (1774).

3. Article 1, section 8, subsection 8.

4. 33 U.S. 591 (8 Pet.) (1834).

5. 347 U.S. 201 (1954).

6. Feist Publications, Inc. v. Rural Telephone Service Company, Inc., 499 U.S. 340, 111 S.Ct. 1282 (1991).

7. 9 Fed. Cas. 342, No. 4, 901.

8. 471 U.S. 539, at 564 (1985).

9. See, for instance, Salinger v. Random House, 811 F.2d 90 (1987); New Era Publishing v. Henry Holt & Co., 873 F.2d 576 (1989); New Era Publishing v. Carol Pub. Co., 904 F.2d 152 (1990).

10. Public Law 102-492, October 24, 1992.

11. Encyclopedia Britannica Educational Corp. v. Crooks, 542 F.Supp. 1156 (1982).

12. Harper and Row Publishers, Inc. v. Nation Enterprises, 471 U.S. 539 (1985).

13. *Congressional Record* (Daily Edition), vol. 122, no. 143, September 21, 1976, p. H10727.

14. *Congressional Record* (Daily Edition), vol. 122, no. 144, September 22, 1976, p. H10875.

15. 37 C.F.R. 201.14.

16. Public Law 102-307, June 26, 1992.

17. 37 C.F.R. 201.24.

18. *Congressional Record*, vol. 127 part 18, October 14, 1981, p. P24049.

Index of Cases

A Book Named "John Cleland's Memoirs of a Woman of Pleasure" v. Attorney General of Massachusetts, 124
Adair v. United States, 99 n. 1
Adelphi University, 92
American Library Association v. Barr, 134 n. 28
American Library Association v. Thornburgh, 128–29
Anamag, 93
Anderson v. Phillips Petroleum Co., 75 n. 86
Ansonia Board of Education v. Philbrook, 71 n. 12
Arnold v. City of Seminole, Okl., 73 n. 55
Arritt v. Grisell, 74 n. 77

Ball v. Kerrville Independent School Dist., 115 n. 9
Bazemore v. Friday, 72 n. 28
Bennett v. Corroon & Black Corp., 73 n. 54
Bethel School District No. 403 v. Fraser, 134 n. 30
Bicknell v. Vergennes Union High School Board of Directors, 134 n. 35
Board of Education v. Pico, 131
Boire v. Greyhound Corp., 101 n. 38
Bolling v. Sharpe, 101 n. 24
Bratt v. International Business Machines, 112
Briggs v. Northern Muskegan Police Department, 109
Butler v. Michigan, 119, 123, 124
Buzogany v. Roller Bearing Co., 75 n. 85

Cary v. Board of Education, 134 n. 34
Chamberline v. 101 Realty, 72 n. 35
Chaplinsky v. New Hampshire, 122, 123
Chapman v. Detroit, 74 n. 66

Childs v. Williams, 112
Cleary v. American Airlines, Inc., 81
Cochran v. St. Louis Preparatory Seminary, 74 n. 64
Coleman v. Jiffy June Farms, Inc., 71 n. 5
Commonwealth of Pennsylvania v. Gordon, 123
Coppage v. Kansas, 99 n. 1
Corning Glass Works v. Brennan, 71 n. 3
Corp. of the Presiding Bishop v. Amos, 30

Delaware State College v. Ricks, 72 n. 27
Detroit College of Business, 92
Donaldson v. Beckett, 137

Earnhardt v. Puerto Rico, 71 n. 18
East Hartford Education Assn. v. Board of Education of the Town of East Hartford, 115 n. 6
EEOC v. Georgia Pacific Corp., 72 n. 22
EEOC v. Manchester East Catholic Regional School Bd, 74 n. 65
EEOC v. Missouri State Highway Patrol, 74 n. 77
EEOC v. Sage Realty Corp., 73 n. 51
EEOC v. University of Detroit, 72 n. 27
Encyclopaedia Britannica Educational Corp. v. Crooks, 159 n. 11
Epperson v. Arkansas, 134 n. 39
Evans v. Mail Handlers, 73 n. 40

Feist Publications, Inc. v. Rural Telephone Service Co., Inc., 159 n. 6
Foley v. Interactive Data Corp., 81
Folsom v. Marsh, 144
Fortune v. National Cash Register Co., 81

Gallegos v. Phipps, 16 n. 5
Gault, In re, 134 n. 29

Geary v. United States Steel Corp., 100 n. 8

Ginsberg v. New York, 125

Glover v. Eastern Nebraska Community Office of Retardation, 116 n. 28

Griggs v. Duke Power Co., 32

Griswold v. Connecticut, 103

Grove Press, Inc. v. Christenberry, 133 n. 9

Hahn v. Buffalo, 74 n. 77

Hall v. Gus Construction Co., 73 n. 44

Harper & Row v. Nation Enterprises, 145

Harris v. Forklift Systems, Inc., 72 n. 36

Harris v. Mechanicsville Cent. School District 382, 134 n. 34

Haskell v. Kaman Corp., 74 n. 73

Hawkins v. Anheuser-Busch, Inc., 72 n. 23

Hazelwood School District v. Kuhlmeier, 132, 134 n. 30

Helle v. Landmark, Inc., 100 n. 15

Henson v. Dundee, 73 n. 45

Hicks v. Gates Rubber Co., 44

Hirshfield v. New Mexico Corrections Dept., 73 n. 60

Hodgson v. First Fed. Savings and Loan Ass'n of Broward County, Fla., 74 n. 71

Holden v. Owens-Illinois, 75 n. 89

Hollenbaugh v. Carnegie Free Library, 108

Howard v. Daiichiya-Love's Bakery, Inc., 74 n. 68

Interstate Circuit, Inc. v. City of Dallas, 133 n. 14

Jacobellis v. Ohio, 127

Jennings v. Tinley Park Community Consolidated School Dist. No. 146, 75 n. 88

Jones v. Janesville, 74 n. 67

K Mart Corp. v. Ponsock, 101 n. 23

Katz v. United States, 115 n. 15

Keppler v. Hinsdale Township High School Dist., 73 n. 40

Kessler v. Equity Management, Inc., 100 n. 11

Laffey v. Northwest Airlines, Inc., 71 n. 1

Laidlaw Corp. v. NLRB, 102 n. 42

Lander v. Lujan, 74 n. 80

Lanigan v. Bartlett & Co., 115 n. 8

Leedom v. International Brotherhood of Electrical Workers, 101 n. 39

Leedom v. Kyne, 101 n. 38

Loeb v. Textron, Inc., 74 n. 79

Marshall v. St. John Valley Security Home, 23

Mazur v. Stein, 140

McCarthy v. Philadelphia Civil Services Commission, 115 n. 10

McDonnell Douglas Corp. v. Green, 31, 51

McGann v. H & H Music Company, 100 n. 17

McLaughlin v. Richland Shoe Co., 71 n. 7

Meritor Savings Bank v. Vinson, 38, 39, 40, 44

Merwine v. Board of Trustees, 72 n. 22

Meyer v. Nebraska, 130

Miller v. Aluminum Co. of America, 73 n. 49

Miller v. California, 126–27

Minarcini v. Strongsville City School District, 134 nn. 34, 35

Minker v. Baltimore Ann. Conf. of United Methodist Church, 74 n. 64

Monroe v. United Airlines, Inc., 74 n. 81

Montgomery Ward & Co. v. NLRB, 102 n. 44

Morgan v. Hertz, 73 n. 46

Mozert v. Hawkins County Public Schools, 130

National Treasury Employees' Union v. Von Raab, 115 n. 19

Naton v. Bank of Cal., 74 n. 71

Neville v. Taft Broadcasting Co., 72 n. 34

New Era Publishing v. Henry Holt & Co., 159 n. 9

New Era Publishing v. Carol Publishing Co., 158 n. 9

New York v. Ferber, 133 n. 24

New York University, 92

Newman v. Legal Services Corp., 100 n. 13

NLRB v. Erie Register Corp., 102 n.43

NLRB v. First Union Management Corp., 101 n. 31

NLRB v. Jones and Laughlin Steel Corp., 100 n. 3

NLRB v. Yeshiva University, 91, 101 n. 30

O'Connor v. Ortega, 110
Oneita Knitting Mills v. NLRB, 102 n. 45
Oscar Mayer v. Evans, 74 n. 70

Palsgraf v. Long Island R.R., 3
Parducci v. Rutland, 134 n. 34
Paris Adult Theatre I v. Slaton, 133 n. 19
Passer v. American Chemical Soc., 75 n. 87
Payne v. Rosendel, 100 n. 9
Peterman v. International Brotherhood of
     Teamsters, 100 n. 10
Pettway v. American Cast Iron Pipe Co.,
     75 n. 86
Phillips v. Smalley Maintenance Services,
     Inc., 73 n. 39
Pierce v. Ortho Pharmaceutical Corp., 100
     n. 7
Pine River State Bank v. Mettille, 100 n. 15
Pope v. Illinois, 127
Pratt v. Independent School District, 134 n. 34
President and Directors, Georgetown College
     of Georgetown University, 101 n. 29
President's Council, Dist. 25 v. Commun-
     ity School Board, 134 n. 35

Queen v. Read, 132 n. 1

Reeb v. Economic Opportunity Atlanta,
     Inc., 72 n. 26
Reed v. Shepard, 73 n. 47
Regina v. Hicklin, 119
Rendall-Baker v. Kohn, 83
Rex v. Curll, 118
Rice v. St. Louis, 72 n. 22
Right to Read Defense Committee v. School
     Committee of Chelsea, 134 n. 35
Ritchie v. Walker Mfg. Co., 115 n. 21
Ritter v. Mt. St. Mary's College, 74 n. 65
Roberts v. Gadsden Memorial Hospital,
     72 n. 29
Robinson v. Jacksonville Shipyards, Inc., 43
Roland v. Christian, 8
Roth v. United States, 123

Salinger v. Random House, 159 n. 9
Salvail v. Nashua Board of Education, 134
     n. 35
Sardigal v. St. Louis Nat. Stockyards Co.,
     73 n. 52
Shapiro v. Wells Fargo Realty Advisors,
     100 n. 21

Sheck v. Baileyville School Committee,
     134 n. 35
Skinner v. Railway Labor Executives
     Ass'n, 115 n. 18
Southland Paper Mills, Inc., 101 n. 41
Spagnuolo v. Whirlpool, 74 n. 80
Stanley v. Georgia, 125
Suchodolski v. Michigan Consolidated
     Gas Co., 100 n. 12
Swayne v. Connecticut, 16 n. 1
Swentek v. USAir, Inc., 73 n. 38

Tardiff v. Quinn, 115 n. 7
Texas Dept. of Community Affairs v. Bur-
     dine, 51
Thurber v. Jack Reilly's, Inc., 73 n. 63
Tinker v. Des Moines Independent Com-
     munity School Dist., 134 n. 30
Toussaint v. Blue Cross and Blue Shield of
     Michigan, 80
Townsend v. Nassau County Medical Cen-
     ter, 72 n. 22
Trans World Airlines, Inc. v. Hardison, 29
Trans World Airlines, Inc. v. Thurston, 25
Tunis v. Corning Glass Works, 73 n. 60

United States v. Bennett, 119
United States v. Kennerly, 133 n. 6
United States v. One Book Called "Ulys-
     ses," 121
United States v. Orito, 133 n. 19
United States v. 12 200-ft. Reel Film, 133
     n. 19

Walls v. Mississippi State Dept. of Public
     Welfare, 72 n. 22
Walter v. KFGO Radio, 73 n. 43
West Coast Hotel v. Parish, 100 n. 3
West Virginia State Board of Education v.
     Barnette, 134 n. 40
Wheaton v. Peters, 138
Williams v. Saxby, 72 n. 30
Williams v. Civiletti, 73 n. 41
Winters v. New York, 123
Wisconsin v. Yoder, 130
Woods v. Safeway Stores, Inc., 115 n. 9
Wooley v. Hoffman-LaRoche, 113
Worthington, In Re, 119

Zykan v. Warsaw Community School Corp.,
     134 n. 34

General Index

Age Discrimination in Employment Act
  Advertisements as violating, 45
  Age groups protected by, 45–46
  Attorneys' fees, 54–55
  Back pay, 53
  Bona fide occupational qualification (BFOQ), 51
  Charge
    Defined, 49
    Time to file, 49
  Coverage, 46
  Disparate impact, 51
  Disparate treatment, 51
  EEOC
    Role, 49–50
    Suit, 50
  Employer, 46
  Employment agencies, 46
  Enforcement procedures, 48–49
  Front pay, 54
  History, 45
  Intent, establishing
    Statistical evidence, 51
    Test requirements, 50
  Labor organizations, 46
  Opposition, 55
  Prima facie case outlined, 51
  Private clubs, 47
  Protections, 47
  Reasonable factors other than age (RFOA), 51
  Reinstatement, 54
  Religious organizations, 47
  Remedies
    Attorneys' fees, 54–55
    Back pay, 53
    Front pay, 54
    Reinstatement, 54
  Retaliation, 55
  Statute of limitations, 49
Americans with Disabilities Act
  ADAAG, 67
  Alterations, 68
  Alternative dispute resolution, 70
  Alternative services, 66
  Attorneys' fees, 70
  Auxiliary aids and services, 64
  Barriers, removal of, 65
  Disability defined, 57
  Disabled persons who pose a threat, 62
  Discriminatory acts, 58–59
  Drugs and alcohol, use of, 61–62
  Elevator exception, Title III, 68
  Eleventh Amendment, effect of Act of, 70
  Employee relation to disabled, discrimination on account of, 59
  Employment, 56
  Exclusions, 58
  Major life activities, 57
  Medical exams and inquiries, 61
  Medical records, 61
  New construction, 67
  Notices, requirement of, 62
  "Otherwise qualified" individual, 59
  Policies, practices, procedures, modification of, 64
  Private entity defined, 63
  Public entity, 68
  Public services, 62, 68–70
  Public accommodations defined, 63
  Readily accessible defined, 67
  Reasonable accommodation, Title I, 59, 60
  Reasonable accommodation, Title III, 64
  Relationship to other acts, 56
  Religious qualifications, 62
  Retaliation, 70

Americans with Disabilities Act (*continued*)
Seating in assembly areas, 66
Segregating employees as discrimination, 58
Self-evaluation by public entity, 69
Tests, discriminatory, 61
Third party discrimination, 59
Title I, 56–62
Title II, 62–63, 68–70
Title III, 63–70
UFAS, 67
Undue hardship, 59, 60
Undue burden, Title III, 64

Censorship
Academic freedom, 130
Background, 117
Child Protection and Obscenity Enforcement Act, 128
Community standards, 124, 127
First Amendment, 124
Hicklin test, 119
Home, viewing obscenity in, 125
LAPS test, 126
Obscenity, 118
Patently offensive, 124
Prurience, 124
Public schools, censorship in, 129
Redeeming social value, 124
School libraries, censorship in, 130
School newspapers, 131
School board responsibilities, 130, 131
Variable obscenity, 124
Whole book theory, 120
Copyright
Berne Convention Implementation Act, 142
Blank forms, 140
Classroom use, guidelines for, 146–48
Compilations, 139
Computer software, 152
Copyright requirements
Original authorship, 141
Fixation requirement, 141
Copyright clause of the U.S. Constitution, 137
Copyright notice, 142
Deposit, 143
Derivative works, 139
Duration of copyright, 141–42
Eleventh Amendment, 158

Fair use, 144
First sale doctrine, 153
Fixation requirement, 141
History, 137
Ideas, systems, principles, 140
Infringement relief, 157
Interlibrary loan, 151
Library copying
Published works, 150
Research, for, 150–52
Unpublished works, 150
Materials protected, 139
Moral rights, 143
Music, fair use in education guidelines, 148–49
Notices required, 151, 154
Off-air taping, 155–56
Original authorship, 141
Public performances, 156
Registration, 143
Reserve book use, fair use guidelines, 149
Rights protected, 138
Software licenses, 153
U.S. government works, 140
Unpublished materials, fair use of, 145
Videotapes
Classroom performance, 155
Classroom use, guidelines, 155–56
Off-air taping, 155
Visual artists' rights, 143
Warnings, required, 151, 154

Employment Security
Bargaining unit, 90
Collective bargaining, 86
Contract, union, 96–97
Employment-at-will, 78
Employment-at-will exceptions
Good faith and fair dealing, covenant of, 81
Implied contracts, 79
Oral contracts, 80
Public policy and good faith and fair dealing distinguished, 82
Public policy exceptions, 79
Termination in violation of statutes, 78
Whistleblower protection, 79
Equal protection, 84
Fourteenth Amendment, 82
Labor-Management Relations Act, 87
Landrum-Griffin Act, 88

Managerial employees, 91
National Labor Relations Act, 87
National Labor Relations Board, 87
NLRB jurisdiction, 87
Participative management schemes and
    unions, 93
Procedural due process, 85
Professional employees in bargaining
    units, 90
Public sector collective bargaining, 99
Public sector employment, 82
State action, 93
Strikes, 97–98
Substantive due process, 85
Supervisors, 91–92
Taft-Hartley Act, 87
Union certification, 96
Union contract, 96
Union elections, 96
Unions, organizing
    Authorization signatures, 93
    Elections, 93
    Unfair labor practices, 94
        Discharges and layoffs, 95
        Economic inducements, 96
        Employment terms, changes in, 95
        Interrogation, 94
        No-solicitation rules, 94
        Organizational picketing, 95
        Polls, 94
        Statements, 94
        Surveillance, 94
        Union insignia, wearing of, 95
        Violence, 95
Wagner Act, 87
Equal Pay Act
    Coverage, 18
    Defenses, 21
    EEOC enforcement responsibility, 25
    EEOC regulations, 18
    Employee flexibility, 23
    Enforcement, generally, 24–25
    Equal effort, 20
    Equal skill, 20
    Equal work, 20
    Factors other than sex, 22
    History, 18
    Jury trial, 25
    Merit, 22
    Quantity and quality of work, 22
    Red circle rates, 22

Remedies, 25
Responsibility, 21
Retaliation, 26
Seniority, 21
Shift differential, 23
Statute of limitations, 24
Temporary or part-time work, 23
Title VII, relationship to, 25
Training programs, 23
Wage standard, 24
Willful violations, 25
Working conditions, 21

Premises liability
    Assumption of risk, 12
    Charitable immunity, 11
    Comparative negligence, 12
    Contributory negligence, 11
    Governmental immunity
        Abrogation by state governments, 10
        Discretionary and ministerial duties
            distinguished, 10–11
        Federal Tort Claims Act, 9
        Governmental and proprietary activi-
            ties distinguished, 10
    Intentional torts
        Assault, 15
        Battery, 15
        Defamation, 14
        Harmful instrumentalities, use of, 14
        Shoplifter statutes, 15
    Invitees
        Defined, 7
        Duty to, 8
        Invitation defined, 8
        Obvious dangers, 8
    Last clear chance doctrine, 11
    Licensees
        Canvassers as, 6
        Defined, 6
        Duty to, 7
        Hidden dangers, 7
        Permission, requirement of, 6
    Negligence
        Defenses, 3–4
        Elements of, 2–3
        Fault, 2
        Foreseeability, 3
        Harm requirement, 3
        Proximate cause, 3
    Roland v. Christian, rule of, 8–9

Premises liability (*continued*)
 Sovereign immunity. *See* Governmental immunity (under Premises liability)
 Third parties, acts of, 12
 Trespassers
  Defined, 5
  Duty to, 5
  Duty to render assistance to, 6
  Known trespassers, 5
  Willful or wanton misconduct, 6
Privacy
 AIDS, 113
 Confidentiality legislation, 104
 Confidentiality, promises of, 112
 Dress codes, 105
 Drug testing, 110
 Generally, 103–104
 Medical records, 111
 Off-duty conduct, 107
 Patron confidentiality, 104
 Physician-patient confidentiality, 112
 Residency requirements, 107
 Searches, 109
 Video Privacy Protection Act, 105

Sexual harassment
 Background, 36
 Defined, 37
 Employer liability, 43
 Employer responsibility
  Policies, 44
  Prevention, 45
 Hostile environment, 39
  Analysis, 39
  Nonsexual elements in, 40
  Physical acts, 40
  Pictures, 42
  Provocative clothing, 41
  Reasonable woman, 40
  Violence, 40
  Vulgar language, 41
 Past conduct as evidence, 39

Quid pro quo, 37
Respondeat superior, 44
Unwelcomeness, assessing, 39

Title VII of the Civil Rights Act of 1964
 BFOQ
  Defined, 34
  BFOQ and business necessity distinguished, 34
 Business necessity
  Criminal records, 33
  Educational qualifications, 33
   Unskilled work, 34
  Generally, 32
  Physical qualifications, 32
 Color, 28
 Coverage generally, 27
 Employer defined, 27
 Employment agencies, 27
 Labor organizations, 27
 National origin, 30
 Race, 28
 Religion, 28–29
 Remedies
  Deferral agencies, 35
  EEOC procedures, 35
  EEOC right-to-sue letter, 35
  Time limitations, 35
   Continuing violations, 36
 Sex, 30
 Title VII principles
  Disparate impact, 32
  Disparate treatment, 31
 Unlawful employment practices
  Color, 28
  Generally, 28
  National origin, 30
   "English only" rules, 31
  Race, 28
  Religion, 28–29
   Reasonable accommodation, 29
   Undue hardship, 29
  Sex, 3